MW00336991

Early Praise for Solving for X

It is widely known that arson is among the most difficult crimes to solve. Bob Luckett and a group of conscientious and dedicated outstanding fire service and law enforcement professionals were challenged by a man described as the most notorious serial arsonist in America. Over a two year period citizens and residents of Maryland, Virginia and the District of Columbia were terrorized by the actions of Thomas Anthony Sweatt almost immediately following the apprehension of the DC Snipers. He plead guilty to a multitude of fires in which people were killed and the lives of surviving family forever changed in the aftermath of more than 50 residential fires that were intentionally set. This true crime book shares the experiences of the people on the inside of a very difficult and challenging fire based criminal investigation.

Bob's book provides a unique perspective of their tireless efforts from the discovery of a group of residential fires (where the source of ignition is eerily similar), formulation of a multi-agency local, state and federal Task Force, on scene actions, laboratory analysis, sleepless nights, the exhilaration of the arrest, confession, court proceedings and much more.

Ron Blackwell
Fire Chief (retired)
Prince George's County Maryland Fire and Rescue

Bob manages to capture the grinding frustration of a long-term investigation as well as the attention to detail that transformed that frustration into a successful prosecution. *Solving for X* is an important read for arson investigators, but also just a fascinating tale of perseverance and justice for everyone.

Jim Trusty
Federal prosecutor who prosecuted the Sweatt case

Early Praise for Solving for X

In *Solving for X*, you will experience the intense pressure investigators working the DC Area Arsonist Case were under as they worked day and night for many months to identify and apprehend the individual responsible for setting fires, primarily in residential neighborhoods, often producing potentially life-threatening consequences. Once a fire is set, there is no way for the arsonist, those directly impacted or responding firefighters to know how the set fire would impact the entire community.

Bob brings you inside the day-to-day working, deliberations and activities of the Task Force with stunning detail, including the many highs and lows experienced, as they diligently worked to solve one of the most significant arson cases in United States history. Everyone has something to glean from Bob's firsthand account of the remarkable collective efforts, while meeting the formidable challenges presented by the treacherous actions of the DC Area Arsonist. Bob also provides a glimpse into the behavior of other well-known arsonists.

After nearly two years of exceptional and painstaking hard work, Thomas Anthony Sweatt was arrested and ultimately convicted of several charges related to setting numerous fires in the Washington, DC area. The specifics of Task Force activities leading to the arrest and conviction of Thomas Sweatt are fascinating as are the personal interactions of Task Force members and others who participated in this massive investigation.

Following his arrest in April of 2005, Bob and his fellow Task Force members spent several days with Sweatt. He explains, in considerable detail, the interviews and interactions with Thomas Sweatt. The rapport and relationship Bob and other investigators established with Sweatt provide a rare and fascinating look inside the mind of a serial arsonist.

William E. Barnard,
Maryland State Fire Marshal during the Sweatt Case (retired)

SOLVING FOR X:

Tracking the
DC Serial Arsonist

An Inside Look
at the Investigation That Captured
Thomas Anthony Sweatt

Federal Case #76010-030065

ROBERT M. LUCKETT

Copyright © 2018 Robert M. Luckett

All rights reserved.

ISBN 978-1-62806-330-1   (print | paperback)

Library of Congress Control Number 2021917520

Published by Salt Water Media
29 Broad Street, Suite 104
Berlin, MD 21811
www.saltwatermedia.com

Cover design: cover image courtesy of unsplash.com user Stephen Radford with design by Salt Water Media

Interior images provided by the author, the DC Arson Task Force, and Jason Pittman | One map created by David Dilts used under Creative Commons

To Mike Conner, Charlie Robertson and Billy Folger: thank you for encouraging me to take a chance and tell a story that needed telling.

To Scott Fulkerson and Tom Daley: thank you for your friendship, direction and support.

To the men and women who were a part of this investigation: thank you for your dedication and work.

To Jason Pittman: thank you for your support, ideas and mentoring.

To my intern, Jessica Wynne: your work and assistance to me has been beyond compare. You have the world at your feet. Go get whatever you want.

To my wife, Caryn Luckett: you are my rock and best friend and I thank you for your unfailing support and encouragement.

To those who go into the darkness to keep others safe

CONTENTS

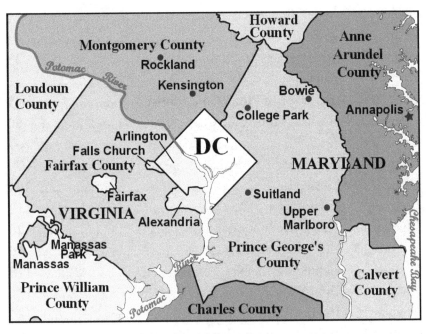

Map of the region
Map courtesy of Wiki Family History David Dilts (DiltsGD)

AUTHOR'S NOTE

Some names have been changed to protect identities.

Conversations and statements are my recollection and
dialogue is not meant to represent exact interactions.

For Prince George's County, I frequently use "PG"
since this is how we typically referred to it.

Task Force Logo
Image from author's files

FOREWORD

On June 6, 2005, Thomas Anthony Sweatt appeared before a United States Federal Court and admitted guilt for more than 300 fires that had wrought terror and angst in two states and the District of Columbia. Sweatt, a loner in his fifties, set fire to vehicles, occupied residential properties, businesses and military recruitment stations. Four people were killed, and a staggering loss of both security and property was left in his wake. His reign of terror lasted for almost two years.

Bob Luckett, chief deputy fire marshal for the Alexandria Virginia Fire Department, was assigned to the Maryland Virginia District of Columbia Arson Task Force after Sweatt set fire to an occupied residential property in Alexandria. The Task Force was a group of more than fifty conscientious and dedicated public safety professionals representing more than a dozen local, state and federal fire and law enforcement agencies. They were determined to identify and bring to justice the person that had been described as the "most notorious arsonist in America."

In this book, Bob has captured the challenges and excitement of a prolific manhunt and ultimate capture of Thomas Sweatt. He describes the extraordinary cooperation, energy and frustrations of the professionals involved in the manhunt as fear gripped a multi-state region. His insights are entertaining and thought-provoking. He generously shares his experience about the inner workings of an arson task force, some of the lessons learned, what takes place after the fire is extinguished and a major multi-jurisdictional fire investigation begins. The book provides a unique perspective on the tireless efforts of investigators, from discovery of a group of residential fires with an eerily similar ignition source to the formulation of the task force, to the sleepless nights, scene investigations and laboratory analysis, to the exhilaration of the arrest, confession, and court proceedings.

Bob writes about Thomas Anthony Sweatt, the DC serial arsonist who had been setting fires since his early teens. He tells about what Sweatt did and his motives for doing it. He provides insightful analysis of this most bizarre and dangerous man. Thomas Anthony Sweatt, whose many fires had a devastating impact on several families, among them Patricia Lewis, the granddaughter of Annie Brown. Annie died as a result of a fire set by Sweatt. At a court hearing she said to Sweatt, "Your actions have left a huge void in my family. We haven't been the same. The day you set the fire was my birthday. So instead of spending the day with my mom and grandmother having cake and ice cream, I spent the day in the emergency room at George Washington Hospital, being told that the woman who raised me may not make it through the night."

I was also a member of the Serial Arson Task Force. I take tremendous pride in our work and proudly recommend this book as required reading for members of the fire service, the law enforcement community, public safety advocates, and the general public.

— Ron Blackwell
Prince George's County, Maryland Fire Chief (*Retired*)

CHAPTER 1

The Problem

The courtroom has always held a very distinguished place with me. I guess my parents instilled much of the respect I have. Having been in court so many times to testify in my cases and yes even a few times for traffic-related stuff I did when I was young, the courtroom has had the mystique of importance. I can recall more than 50 years ago standing in front of juvenile court judge Irene Pancoast sitting above me on the bench in her black robe to receive my driver's permit for the first time. I was nervous, scared and in awe of the judicial process.

Sitting in United States District Court on September 12, 2005 that mystique was still present. The federal courtroom was adorned with federal court judges' pictures, the court pews appeared way more polished than most I could remember and when US District Court Judge Deborah K. Chasanow entered in her robe, I stood along with everyone else and again was in awe of the process. Thomas Anthony Sweatt was at the defendant's table dressed in a suit and we all waited to learn what his sentence would be. Sweatt had pleaded guilty to various counts of possession of destructive devices, destruction of buildings by fire resulting in personal injury, possession of destructive devices in furtherance of a crime of violence. Those guilty pleas resulted in him being sentenced for first degree premeditated murder (felony murder) and second degree murder. They resulted in mandatory life sentences with no chance for parole.

The case investigation had started almost two years prior and while I sat there with most of the men and women that had worked the case with me I wondered how we had gotten to this point. I had no idea

1

at that moment how consumed I had become with this case and the impact it would have on the fire investigation world and how my relationship with Sweatt and things he shared with me would be so insightful about one of the most dangerous and bizarre serial arsonists in the history of the United States.

As you read on you will learn not only about the things Sweatt told me and how I have insight on how his mind worked but you will read about the entire case from beginning to end.

*   *   *

June 5, 2003—It was a warm night, but one you could still sleep with the windows open. The eleven o'clock news was airing but everything else in the apartment was dark and still. The only light in the room was from a thirty-two inch TV screen. The news anchor warned the audience that some may find the next story about a fire a bit disturbing and viewer discretion was advised. The sole viewer in the apartment quickly grabbed a leather pouch from the floor and fumbled to pull out a video camera and turn it on. He was eager to see the results of his work. The red monster—fire—was his friend and he really enjoyed being able to set it loose.

"It took place at 4:30 this morning as most of us were sleeping comfortably in our beds," the news anchor said. "The quiet of this DC night was broken by sirens wailing. Fire units responded to reports of a house fire with people trapped at 2800 Evarts Street. The first arriving units found a white frame house on the corner lot, protected by a chain link fence, being swallowed up by thick black, billowing smoke and the glow of orange flames," he continued. "Crews began pulling hose up flights of concrete stairs to reach the front of the home where the fire was located. Another crew entered the rear of the house and began the search for anyone trapped."

The lonely viewer of the story turned the volume up and moved the camera closer to capture the video of firemen cleaning up the damaged home, now wrapped in gray clouds of smoke.

The news anchor continued: "The crackle of the radio breaks the chaos as the interior crew reports they found a victim in a second floor bedroom. The adult female was quickly removed to waiting paramedics who immediately began life saving measures."

Lou Edna Jones, an eighty-six-year-old female was fighting for her life.

"We will have more on this story right after this break."

The viewer could hardly contain himself. He imagined a firefighter being interviewed, sweaty and tired from fighting the flames created for them; he imagined fire engines racing to the scene.

This could provide some fantastic footage for my next porn movie, the arsonist thought.

The sexy Metro bus driver he had seen go in and out of the house earlier that day had him thinking about the things he could do to that fine-looking man that caused him to get an erection.

The arsonist's second thoughts were, *how beautiful the garden flowers were at the home. Perhaps I shouldn't have spent so much time sitting on the steps and admiring them. Someone could have seen me.* These thoughts quickly disappeared when he played back the video to ensure he had gotten all the juicy footage.

After the commercial, the news anchor told viewers that DC had experienced a few similar fires and reporters would be working with investigators to bring them additional information so they could help in finding those responsible. The arsonist wondered, *what information this reporter might have and if he could use it in my video workshop. He made a mental note to watch the eleven o'clock news the next several days in hopes of seeing more exciting stuff.*

Across the area there were other interested viewers thinking over what had just been reported. In my family room surrounded by all my sports memorabelia and sitting on my well-worn couch sipping a cold one, I was one of those viewers and was hoping that my city wouldn't experience any of these fires. I knew I would lay in bed thinking about this long after I should have been asleep, but knew if we did, then I would be under a great deal of pressure. The politicians would want the case closed quickly and I would be thinking of ways my staff could catch those responsible.

Another interested viewer, an investigator with the Prince George's County, Maryland fire marshal's office, was lying in bed next to his wife watching the news like he did most nights. His wife reading a book by the light of a bed lamp and he propped up by several pillows. He had seen similar fires over the past few weeks. He had passed the information up the chain of command but had not heard anything back. He prayed this news story would change that. His prayers were answered but not quite how he had hoped. He may have started the investigation on these fires in Prince George's County but he would no longer be a part of the case. He was transferred before he could do anything more.

This was only the start of a string of changes that began with a simple promotional exam process. Investigators involved in that process were in a morning bullshit session. Drinking bad coffee and filling up on stale doughnuts and bagels. Everyone standing around and talking about the easy things like weather, sports, and who they knew in common. Investigators from PG and DC were comparing notes. Both departments fight several fires every day. This BS session quickly grew serious when they realized that both jurisdictions were experiencing the same type of fires.

The similarities involving the fires included the following: they had all taken place in the early morning hours, between 0200 and 0600, were all at single-family homes, were all near an exit door—either front or back—were all in the same type of working-class neighborhoods and all the locations were occupied.

Fires happen every day around the nation and one of the main things investigators look for are common traits. If you are skilled and have some great training and experience, you can find one or two. These fires presented several and some were potential problems. Having fires near an entrance or exit, and those structures being occupied, presented real concern for loss of life. With this information in hand, both Prince George's County and Washington, DC, fire investigators agreed to re-examine their previously collected evidence, photographs, and even revisit the scenes. Each would look at what they had and report back to each other in a few days to see if there was any other information to exchange. In the meantime, Prince George's County decided to look much closer at all their fires, using their specially trained accelerant detection canine to help determine the presence of combustible liquids.

This re-examination process began to reveal the presence of what appeared to be some type of plastic and a combustible liquid. All the items collected from the fire scenes were then taken to the Bureau of Alcohol Tobacco Firearms and Explosives (ATF) National Laboratory in Ammendale, Maryland.

On June 23, 2003, PG County officials placed a call to the ATF field office in Baltimore, Maryland, asking them to meet about the fires. On the same day, the results of the lab review revealed that at each of the scenes, the plastic found was a type of polyethylene, consistent with some type of plastic container. The combustible liquid found was gasoline, and there was also the presence of a plastic bag and some type of cloth material. While crude, investigators now knew that whoever was setting these fires was using the same materials, and those materials would be something one could use in making some type of device. These items met the definition of an incendiary device under the US criminal code, and as such, these fires were now considered a federal crime.

On June 25, there was another fire. It was a quiet summer night; the only people out this early were normally the newspaper delivery folks and a few that were leaving for work. At 0450 hours, units were dispatched to a single-family home located at 4920 North Capitol Street in DC. The arsonist had not been able to resist the urge to set another fire. This one was on the front porch, near the door in a manner consistent with the other fires, and resulted in a similar damage estimate as the other fires—about $7,000.

Many of these outside fires were not causing a large dollar loss but all the thick black smoke was causing great fear among the victims.

The arsonist wondered what these reporters knew as he scanned the newspapers and watched the late news but nothing was being reported.

I really want to know the information these reporters have, he thought.

Evidence was collected by DC fire investigators and delivered to the ATF national lab. The results of this laboratory examination revealed that the debris was consistent with the incendiary devices recovered from the previous arsons in Prince George's County. The DC fire was determined to be the work of an arsonist. Following this incident, investigators openly wondered if the series of fires were connected and if they were the work of the same person or persons.

After this fire, there was an initial meeting between the two teams of investigators. As a result of that meeting, the Special Agent in Charge (SAC) of the Baltimore field office held a second meeting which included the chiefs of the fire and police departments in PG County, Maryland and Washington, DC. This created very unusual circumstances as there was now local and federal investigators working in the state of Maryland who had a need to work with local and federal investigators working in the District of Columbia, in effect a second state. The District of Columbia is sometimes described as the fifty-first state. Senior leadership from the involved agencies established the Maryland DC Arson Task Force.

The investigators on the Task Force knew they needed more help and additional staff came from DC, PG, and Maryland State Police, as well as Maryland State Fire Marshals, Anne Arundel County Maryland Fire Department, and PG County Sheriff's Office. With this influx of new bodies, investigators needed additional work space and it was eventually provided at the Prince George's County Fire/EMS Cranford Graves Fire Services Building in Lanham, Maryland, the same location as the PG fire investigations unit. A tipline number was established and a process for answering calls put in place.

The Task Force was headed up by four men and one woman: two

ATF agents, Scott Fulkerson and Tom Daley; a captain for PG County
fire investigations named Scott Hoglander; and the sergeant from the
DC fire investigations division, Sylvester (Sly) Gamble. A third ATF
agent, Tijuana Klas, was placed in the records management position,
overseeing the records management items and other task force
members were set up in a training room that PG County provided as
the work room. There were a couple computers and a few phones but
the setup was far from ideal.

PG investigators worked out of a locked office. It was locked to give
them the privacy they needed and because of the criminal investigations
they conducted. Within this same space was another office area that
belonged to the PG supervisors. Task Force commanders shared the
space with them. Anytime a Task Force investigator wanted to confer
with a supervisor, they had to knock on the door and request entry.
While it was not intentional, it created a grunts versus bosses. It was a
problem every day and had to change. The final straw occurred when
a Task Force investigator and a PG investigator got into an argument
about not being given entry in a timely fashion. Supervisors began to
look for a new workspace that day.

Task Force commanders decided during the initial formation
process that any new jurisdiction that came on board would be offered
a position on the command staff. They never felt they would be adding
anyone else because they thought the fires being set would stay within
the boundaries the arsonist was currently setting them in.

The case agent in charge who would be running the entire
investigation and dealing with all the "fun things" that come with the
day-to-day operations of a fifty-member twelve-jurisdiction working
group was Scott Fulkerson from ATF. A tall man who had spent time
in the federal corrections system before becoming a special agent, he
taught me a lot in our two years working the case.

He was a committed family man, a basketball fan who still played
when he could and he had a real passion for justice. At times he
showed flashes of a temper. He needed to show it more often than

he did and more than once I knew he wanted out of his position. Scott had what I believed was the most challenging job in the Task Force. Leadership of a large group of mostly type-A personalities from fire and law enforcement agencies involved with a high profile case required a special person—and that person was Fulkerson. He did an outstanding job! It was a position that not many would enjoy.

When I was asked to join the Task Force, I wanted to make a good impression on him; the guy was going to be my boss. We went to lunch and talked, trying to get a feel for each other. We talked about our professional backgrounds, some others we knew in the service, where we grew up, went to school, hobbies, and families. It was like we were on our first date and needed to know if we were going to be a good match or not. I liked Scott and felt we would work together well.

Our assistant case agent was Tom Daley. A tall, red-headed Irishman from Philadelphia who came from a long line of law enforcement, Tom brought over twenty years of experience doing fire investigations to the table. He told me his dad walked a beat for thirty years in Philly. Tom was, as the late ESPN broadcaster Stuart Scott would say, "as cool as the other side of the pillow." He was unflappable, even-tempered, and a real professional. He would become a very close friend and confidant during the investigation. He was our most even-tempered commander. He was given the nickname Harry Potter because of the way he handled a meeting with the director of ATF that I could not believe, and he also developed the "flavor of the day theory." The guy was in his forties and still thinking he could row a shell with the best young talents on the water today, but I'm not convinced he knew an oar from a paddle.

I met Daley about two years prior to this case. ATF was working a case involving a fire intentionally set in a commercial building in Alexandria, Virginia, back in the early seventies. After doing some digging on the case, I was able to locate an old file containing some pictures and names. Interestingly enough, a couple of the names in the file were of people I knew. One was a guy I had worked for at a men's clothing firm, and another was a guy who I had gone to high school with. Daley and I tracked these people down and interviewed them. He later contacted me when a search warrant was to be served on the home of the suspect in the case and I was able to be part of the warrant team. It was ATF's way of keeping everyone who had worked on the case involved to the very end. It fostered a good team relationship for any future investigations that could come up.

Working with Daley was easy. We talked about life and solved all the world's problems many times.

Scott Hoglander was a captain for PG County fire investigations and was the group supervisor of our evidence section. One not to mince words, he often expressed frustration with elements of the case and the Task Force that were out of his control. Our styles were a bit different and we didn't always see eye to eye, but it never got in our way of getting the job done.

Hoglander was a canine handler, and his dog—a big black lab—became a mascot of sorts, or at least as much of a mascot that a working canine can be. Early in the investigation I remember one time after a very long night, and everyone was feeling very tired, Misty—Hoglander's canine partner—came into the office looking around at all of us and then began to bark. She didn't care how tired we were, she wanted our attention and if we were not going to give it to her, she was going to demand it. I called her over and got the biggest face lick you could imagine.

Sylvester Gamble, the DC sergeant, was a challenging read. When he was present, he seemed to work hard and appeared fully invested in our work. However, there were times when he was absent for key discussions and decisions, and not seen for days at a time. I knew he was being pulled in many directions by his department, which made it hard on him, but he never allowed himself to become fully engaged in what we were trying to do. In the end, he left the investigation and was never replaced; many still harbor ill feelings for his lack of focus and his poor attitude. I wanted to like him and never understood why everyone called him Sly until after he was gone. We would often drink coffee together in the mornings he showed up. I could tell there was a rub with some of the other folks, and I wanted to get to know him for myself. He was just a guy doing a job. I was never really sure why. I think he was more interested in making a name for himself than making cases.

Our records management special agent was Tijuana Klas. Records management is a crucial factor in all investigations and she was the lifeline to all that we did. A friendly person with an easy smile and a kind word, "T" was the conduit to every facet of the Task Force and the investigative process. She had not been in law enforcement long but you could tell early on that this woman would have a long and stellar career. She had great investigative savvy and people found talking to her easy. When there was someone difficult that needed to be talked with, Klas was charged with getting it done.

The person supervising the entire case was Theresa, the special agent in charge (SAC) of the Baltimore ATF field office, and she was outstanding. She was knowledgeable, professional, and a true advocate for everyone involved in the case. She never let anyone step on us and always worked to keep the heat off by talking to administrators, dealing with the media, and handling issues from behind the scenes. Her involvement in resource acquisition, strategy, and staffing was a sight to behold. We got it done because she got it done.

It did not take long for the case to see its first major change. Lou Edna Jones, the eighty-six-year-old lady that had been rescued from the fire at 2800 Evarts Street in Washington, DC, died.

The case was now considered a homicide investigation.

Investigators found themselves dealing with this new development as well as getting the newly formed Task Force fully operational. There were fires happening everyday in both jurisdictions and they were going to have to figure out a way to have coverage in both areas. The homicide would be adding additional pressure on everyone to close the case before someone else was killed.

CHAPTER 2
My Building Blocks

I would get involved with the case four months after it began. A fire in Alexandria, Virginia, created a space in the Task Force because a fire in a new jurisdiction allowed them to become members and be offered a slot in the command. I was welcomed into the group and shortly after I joined, a reorganization took place. I became the group supervisor of the investigations section. My team was responsible for on-scene interviews, neighborhood canvasses, tip line leads, video collections, suspect development, surveillance, and an assortment of other things as they were assigned. At the peak of the case there were anywhere from twelve to fifteen investigators from local, state, and federal agencies assigned to the section.

I brought almost thirty years of fire service experience to the table, having done investigations and code enforcement work on and off for about twenty of those years. An overweight man with a very loud mouth, I'm always shooting from the hip. If I think about it, I will say it. Being this way had landed me in a good bit of trouble over the years, but folks know where I stand early on, and right or wrong, I stand behind what I say. I love all sports, but football is my life. I enjoy a good card game and a cold beverage and not necessarily in that order. I'm old school—I believe in getting just as dirty as my team and working until the last person has gone home. I have always worked to make sure my team had the equipment they needed to get the job done and I was not beyond begging to get it.

Many people have had a positive influence on my life in public safety. Many, many years ago someone important to me saw a kid who might be headed for trouble. I was hot tempered and shot my mouth off way too often. I believe I have changed for the better over the course of my life, but in the divided early 1970s, I spoke up when I should have kept my mouth shut and I caused a fair share of trouble. This put me on the radar of our school resource officer. When I was a high school senior, the school resource officer approached me and said, "Young man, you should become a police officer."

"Ha," I laughed at the guy. "Me a cop?"

I was way too interested in sports and chasing skirts to become someone who would be trying to help the community and make a positive impact on other young folks. In those days we called school resource officers "Officer Friendly"—they just wanted everyone to get along, and that is how they got their name. Officer Tony Dejerolme was our "Officer Friendly" and he was always talking to me for some unknown reason. I suspect he was trying to keep me out of trouble but I never asked him. Tony knew I was a pretty good athlete, hung with a large group of kids, and didn't worry about causing trouble. I had to learn that you cannot always say what you think.

I'm still learning about this.

I told Tony, "There would be no way I could be a police officer. When a smartass kid like me would run their mouth, I simply would want to beat their tails and that would be the end of it."

Tony just laughed at me and shook his head. You see, Tony was a "cop's cop" and he had earned more awards than I ever knew about. Tony once became involved in a shootout where his partner was shot and was bleeding to death. The pair had responded in the early morning hours to a hole-in-the-wall country bar for a report of a robbery. They were ambushed and his partner took a round very near his femoral artery. Tony made his way to his wounded partner while under fire and stayed in the fight. He sat on the wound to maintain pressure, the entire time staying in the fray and exchanging rounds. Tony was able to slow the bleeding and keep the bad guys pinned down until backup units arrived and got involved. The bad guys were eventually subdued and arrested and his partner transported safely to surgery. Tony was named *Parade Magazine* Officer of the Year for 1974 as a direct result of this shootout.

Tony would not let up on me, "Young man, when you go to the police academy, they will teach you how to tell those smartass kids and adults the correct words and have them saying thank you. You will put them in their place and they will thank you for it."

"Police work is not for me. Way too many rules," I said as I walked away.

When I was twenty-two, I discovered that college was not for me so, I joined the fire department in Alexandria, Virginia, as part of the first paramedic recruit school, and was happy to be making $11,000 a year. I found that I loved helping people and trying to make a positive impact in the community. In the few short years after Tony had approached me, I was starting to understand.

After nine years on the job I had the chance to take a promotional exam to get into the fire marshal's office. I thought if I could get promoted I would enjoy the best job in the world. I could still be in the fire service and be a part of all the of things law enforcement was dealing with: arson, bombings, and hazardous materials. I spent the major part of my career doing code enforcement and fire marshal work. Being assigned to the arson Task Force was the culmination of all that work and I suspect is the reason I felt so strongly about the work we did as a group.

Years later I was working as a deputy fire marshal in Alexandria. Tony was nearing the end of his career and was working as a canine officer. We would see each other occasionally and he told me one time, "Young man, you learned and listened well when you went to the police academy. I hear all the time that you really know how to deal with difficult people. You learned how to tell them what is needed for the situation and have them say thank you when you are finished. You are a man that gets the job done. You are strict, yet fair, and always have the community's best interest in mind with all that you do. Structure and education can be your friend if you allow them to be, correct?"

"Yes sir," I replied. "I wish I had listened to you way back in the day."

Tony not only was a behind-the-scenes mentor to me, he became my friend. I talked with Tony on the phone recently, we talked about how he told me I should become a police officer when I was in high school.

"Bobby, I knew you were a good kid back then and knew you had it in you."

Hearing this was strange for me. Tony and I had been friends for years and he had never said this to me. I had developed into a pretty good investigator and a person who was doing the very things he had told me I would do if I had become a police officer all those years ago. He told me he was proud of the work I had done and that I should be proud of it as well.

"When we met I was only seven or eight years older than you," Tony said, "but I had been to Vietnam and had seen and done way more things than I should have for that age. I could tell that you and most of the kids you hung around were good kids. You just needed time to find your way and not get in trouble before that."

I told Tony that partly because of him, today I still hunger for education; structure is a big part of everything I do. I told him that teaching the younger kids I came in contact with today was very important to me. I want to make a positive impact on them the same way he had on me. I thanked him again for having an interest in a smartass kid and helping show me the right way to do things. Tony told me that nobody had ever expressed this kind of appreciation to him before and it meant alot. There was a silent pause from both of us before we could speak again.

"Tony, you're a good man."

I also had a few important mentors who helped me along when I got started with inspections and investigations. Mike Conner not only taught me as a young paramedic, but took a chance on me as a fire marshal.

Mike had seen me under pressure, dealing with people in a medical crisis, and told me years later that I was a people-person, which was key to being a good investigator. Mike was my best friend and a great boss. His death in 2016 affected me greatly.

Finally, Tom Flynn—Tombo—taught me more about investigations and people than anyone. He was a man that carried himself with honor and respect all the time. He had a quick wit and smile for everyone. I learned a great deal from him about the "Big Red Monster" known as fire. He taught me how it travels, how it burns, the clues it leaves you, and things you need to look for, but Tom taught me even more about people. "Don't judge them, don't degrade them, try to understand them. Your job is seeking the truth and your people skills will help you solve a lot of cases. Never forget, they are just people."

Tombo, I hope I made you proud. I hope you and Mike are raising a pint together today. I miss you guys.

✳   ✳   ✳

The Task Force accomodations in the beginning were good but, as it grew and the days passed, it became awkward, cramped, and difficult. When two investigators had a very heated confrontation—which almost became physical—the space limitations could no longer be ignored. The negative feelings were in place and had to be addressed sooner rather than later. With the Task Force in operation and staff working tirelessly to learn as much as they could about the fires that had already occurred, the day-to-day process was taking shape.

Anytime the Task Force was needed to respond to an incident we were going to be involved, there would be a callout. Callouts were handled in the following manner. Each investigator assigned to the Task Force had their names entered into a database and was paged in the event of a callout request. When paged, investigators would be given the address of the fire and the jurisdiction and asked to respond to that location. They also received a follow-up phone call from their group supervisor.

	A normal day in the task force went like this:
0800 hours	Morning briefing on what was known as well as what occurred overnight. Information sharing from our internal work on images, leads, the media, and surveillance.
1000 hours	Investigators broke off in teams of two and went out on the leads that have been set up from command the night before.
1500 hours	Investigators would return to the office and prepare reports on the leads they had worked that day and discuss the information with commanders.
1700 hours	Some staff would be off duty while others were assigned to standby for a call out or other after normal business hours investigative work.

The command staff began to formulate plans for putting investigators on the street for the overnight hours in which the fires had been occurring, hoping they would be in the area when the arsonist struck again. This caused an interesting problem and one that had been in the news a good bit after the attacks of September, 11, 2001. Communication was on everyone's mind. How would investigators from so many agencies, covering three states, communicate? It would prove to be very difficult. There was no single system available to allow communications to be better at the time. Communication was a major challenge throughout the investigation. Everyone who did not already have one was issued a Nextel phone (a cell phone that also had two-way communications like a walkie-talkie radio) and this is how investigators communicated for the next twenty-two months. Smartphones today have pretty much eliminated this problem. You still need radios that allow your staff to monitor all the traffic in the jurisdictions being affected by the case.

In one instance during our investigations, we were tailing a suspect and I had eight or nine investigators in vehicles trying to keep track of this guy's every move. Murphy's Law came to bear on us and everything that could go wrong did, and at a time when we could not afford it. The suspect did not follow his normal routine. Most of the team lost sight of him. The only person to keep the eye going was a federal agent from West Virginia. Now, West Virginia did not have Nextel, so for me to communicate with him, I had to make a long distance phone call each time I needed information. I would call, talk to him, then disconnect, before connecting directly with the rest of my group. I used up three batteries per day.

During planning sessions, supervisors developed a process on how to handle and collect evidence. This would prove to be a very important part of the investigation. Every time the Task Force would be called to a scene there would be the same group of people identified to handle the process. The evidence team would meet with the investigators in whatever jurisdiction the fire occurred and reviewed the evidence with those investigators.

The host jurisdiction would then dig through the fire debris and collect whatever evidence they felt was needed and turn it over to the Task Force group, who would then transport everything collected to the ATF lab.

This process provided order and consistency and insured continuity with the chain of custody. When there are multiple people from multiple agencies handling evidence the chain of custody becomes vital to your case success in court. You have to be able to show every person that handled it, transported it, and did any type of review or work with it. This also allowed the host jurisdiction to remain the lead in the fire investigation.

The strategy had two parts. First, it ensured that every scene was reviewed by the same set of investigators, thus allowing the Task Force to know each and every time just what they had, and that every piece of evidence was handled in the same fashion each time. Second, it allowed the host agency to remain involved in the investigation so they could work it from start to finish without the Task Force taking over. With very few exceptions, this process proved outstanding.

A large part of the credit for the success of this evidence collection has to go to one person: the person who did all the collections. Tony Exline, was a techno-evidence guy. He was a firefighter, selected to serve as an evidence technician in the fire marshal's office in Prince George's County. This man never said "no." He knew what the evidence was from every scene and kept all the information in his head. He could answer your question before you finished asking. He worked wonders with computers, cameras, and anything that was a machine, but he was not the typical tech guy with pocket protectors and glasses. A hard worker that worked tirelessly and drew very little attention to himself, he was the hardest working guy in the unit, and more than likely the least appreciated because he was never seen unless you needed him.

Exline worked more hours than anyone in the unit. He was at every scene and somehow managed to never miss family events. I'm not sure how he did it, but it was very important to him that his family knew they were just as important as his job. He could walk up to a scene and within just a few minutes of looking it over tell you if this was going to be a job for the Task Force or handled by the affected jurisdiction.

Never forget to appreciate these types of people on your investigation team and more importantly be sure to include them on your investigation team. Investigation units cannot do the job correctly without them.

CHAPTER 3

The Equation

Before the formation of the Task Force, twenty-two fires had been set, and now all the evidence which had been previously collected would need to be reviewed a second time to see if those incidents would be part of the investigation. This would present problems for the entire team as well as those assigned to the evidence section.

While sitting in their cramped office, Scott, the Task Force leader, turned to his second-in-command and said, "Tom, going back and looking at all the previously collected evidence is going to be a real pain in the ass. There are going to be issues. We have to be extra sure that everything and everyone looking at the evidence is recording it on the chain of custody reports. They will need to be updated in a timely manner."

"With so much fire activity in both DC and PG, the evidence team is going to be working way beyond a regular eight-hour day," Tom said.

"Daley, I understand that," Scott said, "but if our process is to remain the same, they will have to be involved in all of the scene and physical evidence reviews. I don't care how long it takes or how many hours they have to work."

"Fulkerson, you kiss butt way better than me and you are going to be doing a lot of that to get this project done. I guess that's why you get paid the big bucks."

"Daley, you can shut up just about anytime now," Scott replied.

Overtime was an issue for every agency during the investigation even though ATF was picking up the tab for just about all of it.

The jurisdictions were upset at the number of hours their staff were working. It really boiled down to the fact they wanted them back working in their department and not working with the Task Force. Dealing with administrators while trying to investigate this case made Fulkerson's job as the Task Force leader even more difficult.

June 30, 2003 was another warm night; it was humid and at 0357 hours the first formal callout to all the newly assigned staff took place for a fire at 2505 Randolph Street in DC. The fire had been set on the front porch near the door. Twelve investigators and the four commanders responded. While there were a few sleepy heads in the group, there was a buzz of excitement among the team; everyone was looking forward to tracking the arsonist down. The scene investigation went well; everyone carried out the tasks that needed to get done and command staff knew they had a process in place that worked. Interviews were conducted and information surfaced that someone was seen riding away from the fire on a dark-colored mountain bike.

The first callout and a promising piece of information had been obtained. Prior to this, PG and DC were doing separate investigations and handling it the way each agency normally did. Now, there would be a bunch of calls made to several people in different agencies to ensure that everyone involved would respond.

Daley, Hoglander, and Fulkerson talked at the scene and they knew making the calls for every fire and then expecting a proper response was going to be interesting. They would have to work on that. Right now they needed to find the person who provided the information about a dark-complected male in a burgundy shirt, dark pants and wearing a blue baseball cap that was seen riding away from the scene on a bike. A sketch was needed to be made so it could go out via the press. This was a critical witness.

*   *   *

The July 4th holiday is coming up. I wish I had someone to enjoy all the activities with. It becomes harder and harder for me to see all these people with their families having fun. Cooking out, going to watch fireworks and enjoy family time.

The arsonist was becoming more agitated, he wanted all the things that he considered to be normal and didn't yet have any of them. He started driving his car around the streets after work and going late into the night looking for someone to be his. It took him two days to find his next target. It wasn't a person; it was another home. The look of the place suited him. The night was still, the hour was late, and the sun was about to come up.

My firemen needed something to do. It is time to set the red fire monster loose.

The arsonist had been driving his car around for hours; it was 0517 on the second of July, but the driving had been worth it. The target was 316 17th street in Southeast, DC.

The arsonist parked half a block away from the house. As he sat and admired the home he allowed his thoughts to wander. *How great would it be if this fire caused a handsome young black man to come running out into my arms. I would hug him tenderly and show him just how much I could do for his firm muscular body. I would gently kiss his lips and assure him he was safe from the fire.*

The arsonist approached the home very quietly; he did not want any noise to alarm anyone inside. He approached a side porch and placed his device next to the entry door. He looked around, and took a few minutes to admire the home and it's surroundings. He then lit his device and vanished into the darkness.

*   *   *

The callout process worked again and all the evidence was collected and went to the lab. With the Task Force in full operation, things were starting to take shape in terms of forming a possible list of people of interest and how this arsonist was working.

- All the fires were taking place at single-family homes.

- The majority of these homes had exterior vinyl siding.

- This was of interest because it made it more difficult to locate the device among the melted debris. The vinyl burns and melts just like the plastic.

- All the fire locations were located near a green area: park, playground, school. This was of interest because it provided a place of cover or concealment for the arsonist.

- All the fires were taking place in the early morning hours. The earliest was 0056; the latest was 0542 hours. This was of interest because it might indicate the type of person we were looking for. People who work at night between midnight and six in the morning: cab drivers, newspaper carriers, construction workers or others.

- All the devices were the same: one-gallon plastic jug, gasoline, some type of cloth wick, and a plastic bag. This was of interest because investigators could not find any fire departments in the area that had seen set fires where these types of items were found.

- The majority of the fires in Washington, DC were happening in sections called Southeast and the areas in Maryland: District Heights, Capitol Heights, Temple Hills, Oxon Hill, and Suitland—all bordering the District of Columbia and on or near major thoroughfares. This was a possible indicator of the roads that were being traveled. The arsonist was more than likely using the Capital Beltway, which makes a full circle around DC, Maryland, and Virginia and/or Route 295 which runs along the Maryland/DC border in the area of the fires.

While the Task Force had only been operating formally for a few days, they had compiled the information that PG and DC investigators had put together and this was what they used as their starting point.

Who could this person or persons be? The entire Task Force constantly wondered. It never matters what your crime is, how your investigation started, who is assigned, or how long it takes. The work is centered on doing one thing and one thing only the entire time the case is open: solving for x. This became the theme for our work and Daley would remind us each day that this is what we were doing.

The arsonist arrived at his home. He was content. He had set another fire, was able to see his firemen work, and now it was time to masturbate to his fantasy and fall fast asleep.

The Task Force focused on several investigative issues: where might the next fire occur, what should they do next and when should they do it? The Task Force spent the next several weeks learning as much as possible about construction of the device, the fire behavior involving the device, and characteristics of flammable liquids in plastic containers. The ATF National Lab provided a re-creation and mock-up of single family homes that had been targeted. Vinyl siding received a lot of attention and some homes scheduled for demolition were used for fire testing.

A model flammable device was created and included a plastic one-gallon container with gasoline filled to an assortment of levels with a cloth wick. From these real-time tests we found that the flame was relatively small and several minutes passed before a free-burning fire was produced. We also found the device produced heavy black smoke. Once investigators understood how the fires were burning and the type of damage they were doing, they needed to understand more about the device. They continued to analyze the characteristics of the device using video technology. After more than a dozen tests the following information emerged: a 12-to-28 minute period before free-burning occurred and the flame produced was similar to that of a candle, slow moving or lazy flickering. The flame was low and could not be seen

SOLVING FOR X

A recreation of the device is burned at the ATF lab.
(Image courtesy of the author's files)

well. Once the plastic container failed and the gasoline vapors began to burn, the fire burned itself out quickly, consuming the fuel and oxygen that was available, producing a large volume of thick black smoke.

The test raised additional questions. How was someone using gasoline and not burning themselves? Was the arsonist someone who had a good bit of knowledge about fire? Was the arsonist a firefighter?

From my knowledge and experience, I had learned firefighters who set fires generally do not set fires in buildings that are occupied. Would a firefighter know that the thick black smoke caused by this device would normally alert the residents of a home before the fire got too large? Would a firefighter know that the thick black smoke would scare the people more than anything because of the lack of visibility? All the fires had been set near a door, but all the locations had a second means of escape. Would a firefighter know this? Would a firefighter be out at this time of the night or morning? Going or coming from work?

These questions required another series of investigations to be conducted by Task Force members. They learned a lot about the working shifts of firefighters throughout the region. What shifts were on-duty or off-duty during the fires? There is a substantial volunteer firefighter presence in the region. What were the time periods for volunteer participation? Several firefighters were two hatters: working as paid career firefighters in the region and also volunteering while off duty. Were there any particular fire shifts that were off for all the fires? Were there any particular firefighters off for all fires?

Before I became a member of the Task Force, I had thought it a strong possibility that the person setting all these fires could be a firefighter. Thinking it could be someone in the same profession as you is not a pleasant thought. In fact, it is a very shitty thought, but I had seen it many times in the past and knew it would have to be explored at some point. The Task Force didn't know how many of the volunteers were paid in PG, how many worked for DC, or how many of the DC fire personnel were volunteers in PG. These issues proved to be very difficult and were never totally overcome.

There are many cities and towns around the nation that have what are referred to as combination departments. These are departments that have both fully-paid firefighters and volunteers. Most firefighters start as a volunteer in some community. Once they make the decision to become paid in some agency, they do not leave the volunteer community as it is very much needed and many communities around the nation rely solely on volunteer firefighters to provide the service.

After an active June with twelve fires, the trail suddenly went silent. There was a fire on July 2, then no more fires associated with our case until September 2, 2003.

The Task Force shifted its attention to why. Why do the fires stop? New questions were being asked: has the person or persons been killed, gone on vacation, been incarcerated, become bored, moved out of the area?

Questions persisted, and although callouts had all but ceased, the

Task Force remained energized. The lull in fires created concern from some of the agencies involved that those who were assigned may be better utilized if they returned to their normal duty assignments in their home departments and jurisdictions. The regular staff briefings moved from being solely case updates and now included sales pitch conversations around the importance of keeping the same people involved in the case from beginning to end. Since every agency had many things going on and everyone needed more staff, could the Task Force continue at this pace? This would be a question that Task Force administrators would have to answer on a regular basis until the Task Force shut down.

During this time, as fires involving single family homes waned, there was a sudden series of fires in high-rise apartment buildings in DC. Interestingly, the origins and causes had a strong resemblance to the fires being examined by the Task Force. Has our person or persons of interest returned? Could this be the arsonist? Following interviews of potential witnesses and others in or near the apartment buildings experiencing the fires, investigators were able to develop a suspect. This was done by looking at video, doing criminal history checks on folks with criminal backgrounds living in the buildings, and twenty-four hour surveillance. This new development injected additional energy into the Task Force. On July 29, members of the Task Force were on site of the Marina View Towers Apartments gathering information. This location had been the scene of a recent fire incident. While investigators were in the building, another fire occurred. Daley radioed Gamble to meet him in the stairwell on the third floor. When he arrived, Daley and Fulkerson were waiting for him.

"This is fucking unreal. A fire while we are here in the building," Gamble said.

"Scott, do we have enough to arrest this guy?" he asked.

"I don't know just yet," answered Scott.

"You do know that this guy, our suspect, lives in this building, right?" said Gamble.

26

"You should have told me that when you got here. I'm still not sure we can arrest him but we sure have good enough reasons to go and talk with him."

After the fire was declared under control, the three men headed to the suspect's apartment, armed with the following information: this suspect failed to pay rent in a timely manner for several months; he had not been a good neighbor, often involved in conflict with apartment staff and other residents; and not one person they talked to about this guy had anything positive to say about him. In fact, all of them said he was an ass. This did not make him an arsonist, but it did show them he may be capable of doing something like setting a fire. When they knocked on his door, the first thing they noticed when he answered was he had fresh burns on his hands. When they asked him if he was okay or if he needed them to call him an ambulance, he quickly blew them off and said he didn't want anything from them. They were looking around as best as they could to see if anything of use to their investigation was in plain view but this guy was keeping them very near. He was very uncooperative and refused to answer questions. They thanked him for his time and left.

Once in the hall, Fulkerson said to Gamble, "I think now we have enough to arrest him." Gamble was directed to watch the apartment with the rest of the team that had been in the building doing interviews when the fire call happened. Fulkerson and Daley went to obtain an arrest warrant. There was relief among the Task Force members because they thought they had solved the case.

Fifty-seven-year old Paul DuBois was arrested and taken into custody. He was charged by the Superior Court of the District of Columbia with assault with intent to kill, second-degree burglary, obstruction of justice, and arson. A trial was scheduled for April 16, 2004 and everyone was happy. The news story of the arrest made the arsonist happy.

So they have arrested the arsonist. I should be able to set all the fires I want now. Thinking they have the arsonist will make it easier for me to set the red fire monster loose whenever I want.

During the course of the investigation on DuBois, investigators uncovered information that appeared to link him to a double homicide. They turned that information over to the New York State Police. Task Force members began pulling together all the information they had on DuBois preparing for trial. They worked with the property managers to gather the information they had on him while he was living in Marina View Towers. They interviewed his co-workers; they went to New York to try to find out more about the murders. While these investigative steps involved a few team members, the remaining investigators were getting ready for new assignments.

It had been over sixty days and there had been no additional fires. Some thought, *We really do have the guy.*

*   *   *

Thursday, September 4, 2003—almost a month after the DuBois arrest—a fire was set in Prince George's County at a home located at 5101 Barnaby Run Drive in Oxon Hill, Maryland. The fire was reported at 0315 hours. The device was placed near the front door. The Task Force responded and evidence technicians recovered components consistent with our suspect device.

The arsonist was home all comfortable in his bed. Satisfied with his work. He had been waiting a long time to set another fire and see his fireman do their work.

Standing at the scene and looking at things with Fulkerson, Daley made a comment, "Welcome back."

Fulkerson just laughed and said, "Yep."

"We are going to have to go to each agency and kiss ass to get all these people back. I really hate this political BS," Hoglander said.

"We'll let Fulkerson figure that one out. You need to get this evidence to the lab," Daley responded.

The Task Force had been in the early stages of disbanding. They had made an arrest and thought the case was over and now had to re-engage the process of solving for x. Everyone had the feeling of accomplishment, thinking they had solved the arson investigation and then found out that was not the case. In fact, they had not solved a major case, they were still in the middle of it. Tijuana called Fulkerson; she was feeling a great deal of frustration.

"Scott, I just don't know how I'm going to manage getting all these reports and other documents set back up and re-open them for everyone to be able to see. I mean, I know how to do it, but it's just going to be a ton of work and I really don't have the time. You guys just don't have any idea what it takes to get this stuff done," she said.

Fulkerson was quiet for a minute as he gathered his thoughts and then said, "T, you have one of the most difficult jobs on the Task Force. I could not begin to fully understand all that you do and I know the volume of work I and others place on you seems unfair, but you are a genius with this and will get it done. I know it sounds like I'm blowing smoke up your skirt but I'm not."

Tijuana laughed out loud, then said, "I really appreciate your words. I know you well enough to know that you aren't just feeding me a line of BS, but know this! I think this is a bunch of crap."

The frustrations were enormous and it would take everyone a few days to get beyond it. Sixty-plus days since the last fire and now just a few days away from school starting up, again a fire. The Task Force staff had been trying to figure out why the fires had stopped. Could the person or persons setting these fires be connected to schools somehow? A clue to be looked at much closer. One thing for sure, Paul DuBois did not set it. Perhaps it was a copycat.

A supervisors meeting was held to develop some type of plan. Fulkerson and Daley, along with Tijuana and Hoglander, decided they must be ready to catch this person or persons, and they assigned the entire task force to go to night operations.

Investigators were set up in teams of two with part of the command staff covering Maryland and the other covering DC. Fulkerson called Theresa and explained what had been decided. Theresa was the Special

Agent in Charge of the Baltimore, Maryland field office of ATF. She had shoulder length jet black hair, was quick to keep things fun, and generally had a comical comment or great comeback to a smart ass comment, but you better not cross her and she never let anyone try to talk bad about us. He asked her to call the DC Metropolitan Police Department and outline the plan.

After consulting with them, Chief Charles Ramsey made the decision to assign a team of twelve officers from various assignments to work only fires until this person was apprehended. These officers would work the midnight shift. They responded to all fire scenes in DC, and if the fire was one that had been set by the arsonists, they would be on the scene quickly to assist.

Theresa called Scott and reported her good news. "Scott, DC police are on board. They not only will be assisting you, Chief Ramsey has assigned twelve officers to work midnights on this case until it's over."

"Thank you, ma'am. I will get with the midnight watch commander tonight and find out who all the players are. Thanks for your help."

"No problem Scott, and just one more thing."

"Yes ma'am?"

"Go catch whoever is doing this."

Laughing half-heartedly, Fulkerson said, "Will do."

The Task Force, with a staffing boost from the Metropolitan Police, was deployed all across the entire city of DC and PG County in hopes of catching the arsonist in the act of setting another fire. It was Monday, September 8 at 0349 hours, the first day of school for kids in the DC area. It was going to be a nice weather day for the kids, currently in the high sixties with a forecast of sunny and low seventies for the day. The DC fire department responded to the report of a house fire at 202 Quackenbos Street. The first arriving fire crews reported fire on the front porch. Once the fire was declared under control fire crews were concerned the fire may be Task Force related. Members of the Task Force responded and indeed it appeared to be the work of the person or persons believed to be the arsonist. The

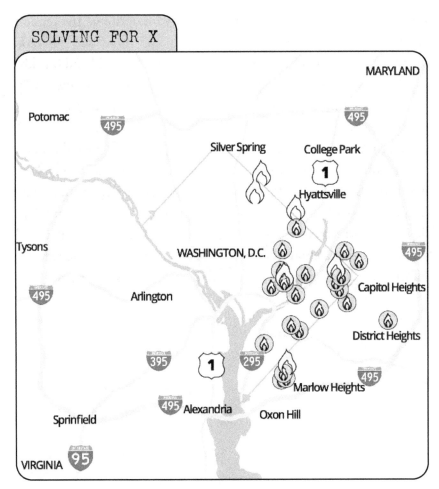

SOLVING FOR X

Updated map. Recent fires highlighted.
(Map courtesy of Jason Pittman)

overnight crews were riding primarily in the Northeast section of DC and this fire took place in Northwest. Fulkerson wondered to himself if someone was telling the arsonist what the Task Force was doing?

The arsonist was active again; this was his second fire in six days. Wednesday, September 10, at 0237 hours, another still early fall night, folks enjoying the last days of comfort before the cold. The fire was set at 4713 Dix Street in Washington, DC, Northeast. The fire was located on the porch at the front door. All the components were present.

Investigators were in the area but came up with nothing. The tension among investigators was starting to build up. There was non-stop media attention and everyone was hoping the case would end quickly.

The Task Force was asking themselves, *Who is the arsonist? Why isn't anyone seeing this person? Why doesn't anyone have information to present to investigators?*

Elected officials, community groups, and neighborhood associations were clamoring for information about the fires. "Why hasn't the Task Force done more to identify someone and share information with everyone?" was the question on the community's lips. Task Force supervisors begin a series of meetings with interested parties and media about the Task Force and its activities. A reward for information leading to the arrest and conviction was increased.

CHAPTER 4
Three Brothers

Sunday, September 14, 2003, at 0929 hours, a concerned citizen called the DC Metropolitan Police. She reported that her sons had encountered a man at about four in the morning and the man left behind some type of jug with something that smelled like gasoline in it. The Task Force was immediately notified and everyone who had been assigned was ordered to respond. The location was 4115 Anacostia Avenue, Northeast. When investigators arrived on the scene they met the lady and her husband, her three sons, and two daughters. Investigators surrounded the home and blocked off the neighborhood streets. The day lasted just a little over fourteen hours. Before it was over the entire area had been gone over with a fine-tooth comb. The ATF mobile lab and DC police mobile crime lab was on the scene to assist. The two primary lab technicians working with the evidence from ATF were called at home, picked up by investigators and brought to the scene. The three boys, Reginald (Reggie), Jerome, and Rickey agreed to be interviewed by investigators; they were separated and taken to the same location to be interviewed.

The three brothers told investigators that they were coming home from work, promoting nightclubs in Washington and nearby Prince George's County, and arrived in the same car at about 0400 hours. As they pulled up to the front of the home, they noticed a man sitting on the front steps. When he saw the car pulling up, he walked down the steps and began to approach the car.

Reggie, in the passenger seat, rolled down his window and the man said he was looking for someone and provided a name.

SOLVING FOR X

Witnesses spotted a man with a container of gasoline sitting on the porch of this home around 0400 hours on September 14, 2003.
(Image courtesy of the author's files)

Reggie and his brothers told the man they didn't know anybody by that name, and the man began to walk away in the opposite direction of their house. The boys decided they wanted to find out more about what this guy was doing so they quickly squared the block and came around to their street. While squaring the block, they decided to use a shortcut and go along the alley to the rear of the home just in case this guy decided to cut through. When they get back to their street it is empty; they do not see the man anywhere and there is no traffic moving. The boys got back to their house and parked, but they still did not hear or see anything. They walked up to the front steps and then saw a car pass in front of their home. They reported that they found some bags on the front porch that contained a one-gallon jug filled with some type of liquid. They also saw some pieces of cloth in the bag. They smelled the liquid and it smelled like gasoline. They quickly entered the home to make sure everything and everyone was okay. All was fine.

They went back to the porch and looked around, everything was quiet and nothing was moving so they discussed what to do.

The three boys believed that the man might have been planning to rob the place or that he was dangerous and was going to blow something up. They decided to dispose of the stuff found on the porch.

There is a school, a park, and a playground directly across the street and the boys decided to put the items they found on their porch in one of the trash cans there. Once the items were discarded they began to talk and decided that putting gasoline in the trash was not a safe idea. They decided to pour the gasoline down the sewer and dump the plastic jug and other items they found on their porch there as well. When the three boys returned home, they stayed up the rest of the night in case the man returned and they remained awake by playing video games. They placed a few calls to their mother, who was away for the night, but she did not answer, so they left her a message and continued to keep vigil.

When she came home in the morning, they told her all that had happened. The mother got a little upset with the boys and asked them if they were aware there was an arsonist in the area and maybe this person was going to set their house on fire. The boys were not aware of the arsonist and reported that their mother became even more upset upon hearing this, and she promptly called the police to report what her sons had told her. Following interviews with the brothers, Daley, Fulkerson and Hoglander had a meeting with the team.

"I think we need a sketch artist to see if we can picture what this guy looks like," said Fulkerson. "Does anyone know the contact for the Maryland State Police who arranged for our bike witness drawing?"

Folger spoke up. "The State Police don't use an artist. They use the EFITS system."

"OK, I stand corrected, do you have any contacts?"

"Yes, sir, I can make a call," he said.

It was decided that a sketch of the person seen by the boys could be of some help. The Task Force made a request to the Maryland State Police for use of the special sketching software.

They used EFITS, Electronic Facial Identification Technique, which creates a drawing of a suspect based on eyewitness observations. When the trooper arrived, he talked with Reggie because he had been in the passenger seat and had the best view of the man. The trooper and Reggie went to one of the command vehicles and set up in front of a computer. The trooper told Reggie to just tell him what he could remember about the man he saw. He began by telling him that as he and his brothers drove up to their house they saw a man sitting on the front steps of their house. The man quickly got up and began to walk towards them. Reggie said he put his window down and the man asked them if they knew a guy by the name Justin. He told the trooper the man looked older but not too old and had a patch of white hair in the front. As he talked the trooper was entering the information in the computer.

"Tell me about his eyes," asked the trooper.

Reggie said, "They were round and sort of big, but not too big."

"Tell me about his nose and mouth," the trooper asked.

"His nose was wider than mine and his lips weren't too big," Reggie replied.

The trooper said, "Thank you, I think I have all I need."

With that, Reggie said, "Cool." And out the door he went.

The Task Force now had a sketch of someone of interest.

Investigators conducted a painstakingly meticulous examination of the scene. They were working on the front porch and knew their daylight and good weather were going to be limited.

The lead forensic scientist of the investigation had responded from home to assist. He brought all the forensic staff and evidence collection people together to discuss the procedures they needed to

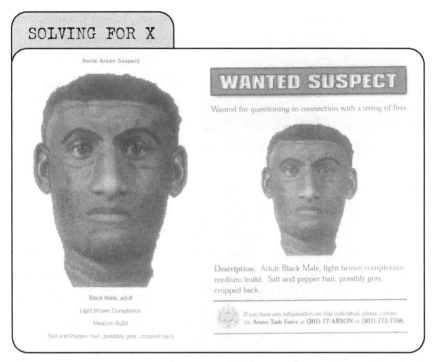

EFITS Sketch. Inset: Wanted suspect poster distributed by the task force. (Image courtesy of the DC Arson Task Force)

get done. Ray Kuk would be our main point of contact for everything evidence and forensic related during the investigation.

After meeting with everyone, it was decided that the best approach would be to build a lean-to to cover and protect the front porch from any approaching weather. The scientists wanted to fume the metal handrails on the steps. Fuming is a process used to develop fingerprints. Super glue is heated and the fumes from that process stick to the oils left by the fingerprints and reveal prints from whomever touched the area that was fumed.

Once the lean-to was built, the team heated the super glue and directed the fumes toward the handrails. They used a flashlight to see any fingerprints that had developed. Prints were seen and lifted using tape and placed on fingerprint cards for further examination. A few possibilities were found.

To allow for a closer examination in the lab, it was decided that both of the metal handrails should be collected. A new set of wooden rails were built and installed.

Investigators then moved to the sewer where the boys said they had dumped stuff. They removed the cap to the sewer and saw they had a four-to-six foot well called a catch basin. The tubes leading to the catch basin were clean and dry so they knew the items in the well had not been disturbed. They removed three bags, one from an area convenience store, known as 7-11, and two white plastic bags with red lettering, The type of bags often called "thank-you" bags. Found in the bags was an empty one-gallon plastic container. The product label was for Arctic Splash fruit punch with a UPC code and sell-by date of October 13. Also present in the bags was a black piece of material with the words CELO SPORTS embroidered on it. All the items were collected and placed in brown paper bags, sealed them with evidence tape, and recorded the date, time, address, and initials of the person who had made the collection. The initials were placed across the tape and onto the bag so anyone could see if the seal had been broken or tampered with. This process would be followed at every scene the Task Force responded to and collected evidence. It was important to be consistent with the collection process so when the case went to court there would be no question about how evidence was collected. All the items collected were then transported to the ATF lab for further examination. After a very long day of interviews, area canvass, gas station visits, and reviewing many, many pages of notes investigators were able to go home.

Monday, September 15, 2003—the day after the reported sighting of the arsonist—the Task Force staff meeting was bustling with information received the previous day. Fulkerson started the meeting at eight o'clock sharp. When he said eight, that is just what he meant.

"I want to start by thanking all of you for your hard work yesterday. I know you were kept away from family on one of your few days off, but I think what we found will go a long way toward helping us solve this case. Tony, could you tell us all the items that were taken to the lab?"

Tony Exline was a firefighter assigned to the Task Force to collect evidence.

"Yes sir, I would be happy to. I won't go into great detail on every item because we would be here all day, but if you have questions feel free to ask me. A one gallon plastic jug filled with gasoline," Tony said.

Billy Folger, an investigator with PG, interrupted, "I have a question about the jug."

"OK," Tony said.

"Do we know what type of product was in the jug before the gas?"

Exline's reply made the room erupt into laughter.

"Folger, if you would have given me half a chance to talk, I would have told you. You are always thinking ahead of everyone. I can't tell you for sure what was in the jug before the gas, but the label on the jug said 'Arctic Splash.' It's a fruit drink sold in most 7-11 convenience stores. Now may I move on?"

"Please, be my guest," Folger said with a smile.

Fulkerson stepped in, "Guys, can we cut the shit? There is a good bit to cover here."

Tony continued, "There were three plastic bags. One was a 7-11 bag and the other two were white with red lettering. A black piece of material was found in one of the bags and had the words CELO SPORTS embroidered on it. The metal handrails which forensics super-glued provided a few sets of partial prints. I have an 1100 hours phone call scheduled with Ray and hope to learn more then."

"Thanks Tony," Scott said. "Daley, please have a couple folks look into the CELO SPORTS piece. We need to know if the material was part of a shirt, jacket or something else. If we could find out where the embroidery was done that would be really good and finally lets learn all we can about what the hell CELO SPORTS is."

"Copy that boss, I'm on it," Daley replied.

Every detail of what the day had brought to the Task Force was covered and the meeting lasted until almost 1000 hours. As a result of the meeting, it was agreed the Task Force would go public with a plea to the arsonist. ATF offered the services of its behavioral sciences unit including profilers. The Task Force brought in a geographic profiler and personal profiler and they generated the following information:

- He may abuse alcohol.
- He may engage in reckless driving or unsafe practices at work.
- He may have a criminal history.
- When things go wrong in his ife, he likely projects blame onto others outside himself. It is never his fault.
- He likely lies a great deal and his dishonesty causes him problems in interpersonal relationships.
- He lacks what would be considered normal empathy or concern for the welfare of others.
- He may work in a minimum wage position.
- He may live close to where the fires are being set.
- He is likely African American.

The above information with the new sketch and an offer of a $25,000 reward was prepared and presented to the public via a very well-attended news conference held at the Prince George's County Fire Services Building. All the local television stations carried the news conference and showed the computer generated picture of the person of interest.

*　　*　　*

The eleven o'clock news was being watched from the living room. The arsonist watched with great pride because they were talking about him.

I didn't even get to set a fire and these people are talking about me. I may just go back to that house and let the red monster loose. Those boys were not very friendly and I sure would enjoy teaching them a lesson.

Those people have not seen the last of my work!

Now there was an image of someone who may resemble the arsonist. The phones started ringing off the hook. Everyone in the public knew someone who looked like the sketch and wanted the money. A year earlier the Washington, DC, Virginia, and Maryland region had been terrorized by the DC Sniper. Now, a little less than a year later, an arsonist was generating tremendous fear and concern in neighborhoods across the region. Some involved believed the sketch had become the Task Force's "white box truck." During the sniper investigation, a witness at one of the early shootings reported seeing a white box truck leaving the area immediately after someone had been shot. The fear created by this reported sighting was difficult to understand. Every white box truck in the DC region was being looked at as belonging to the shooters. This situation had every law enforcement officer involved. I even followed a few and made stops on white box trucks which were sitting in traffic.

The people responsible for those senseless deaths of many people were found in a dark blue sedan and not a white box truck. Was this picture going to be like that or would it really be what the arsonist looked like? Investigators voiced their concern openly.

With all the phone call leads being generated the Task Force now had more work than they could handle, running down all the look-alike leads.

The number of new leads following the release of the person of interest was a blessing and a curse. As the hot line churned out information, more staff was needed and a re-evaluation of the lead management process was on the table. The Task Force developed a new procedure to handle all leads. This process would be followed throughout the remaining time the Task Force was in operation.

Any person listed as a possible suspect would have the following process done to either rule them in or rule them out:

- Obtain a Division of Motor Vehicles picture (if one was on file)

- Run a criminal history check on the name provided
- Interview the caller providing the tip
- Conduct offline checks on the possible suspect's background
- Conduct a wage earnings report
- Conduct a real property search
- Conduct a visual on the established property found to include any vehicles
- Conduct interviews with subjects and rule in or out

While the process itself was outstanding, it did cause a good bit of heartache among staff inside the Task Force.

There was a concern from some that following up on every call may not be the most productive way to proceed. Some believed the Task Force was pursuing leads that had no relation to the case.

For example, a tip would come in that a person they used to work with looked like the picture. When asked when they worked with the person they would say, maybe five years ago. Investigators felt they were wasting their time having to deal with this type of lead.

Everyone was reminded to trust the process. Administrators took these concerns into consideration and established a policy of classifying the look-alike leads as high, medium, or low. This was done so all the leads considered high could be addressed in a more timely fashion, yet still address all the leads in the same manner. For example, leads that came in with "The sketch looks like a person I went to school with ten years ago and I have not seen him since" were placed in the low category.

Daley always took a calming approach to problems.

"Since we just never know when there might be one that would lead us to the correct person, we need to treat each and every person the same. We have to check out everyone and talk to them all no matter what the details are. I hope all you can understand the need here."

Collectively the group said, "We get it."

Many, many hours went into this process over the twenty-two months of the investigation. A total of more than 450 people were part of this potential suspect pool. Supervisors in the Task Force learned early on to listen to their investigators so they could keep them engaged. They learned they not only had to stay in tune with what was going on in the investigation, they had to stay in tune with their people. Every Monday morning, the staff meeting was about keeping the focus on the end result: everyone wanted to catch the person or persons responsible for setting these fires. Things became even more difficult for the Task Force supervisors as they now had to cover the nights and still have staff available to work leads. Staffing was changed, with half working days and half working nights. Supervisors were working both.

Exline and Folger were discussing the new shift assignments and both had great concern.

"My family at home is one of the most important parts of my life," Exline said. "Now I'm going to have to be away even more than usual."

"How do you manage to keep up with all the things that your kids do, Tony?" Folger lasked.

"Billy, a long time ago my wife and I talked about this very thing. I told her before we got married that public safety work creates a tremendous amount of stress in a relationship. I told her they would have to get used to sharing me with the job. It hasn't always been a picnic, but we have managed to make quality time more important than quantity of time."

Folger shook his head and said, "Man, far too often this stuff leads to divorce. Family gets put to the side so we can go and do our jobs. I'm sure glad we got good women."

"Folger, tell me how good your wife is when you tell her about our new schedule."

"Shit, I almost forgot. I still have to do that. No worries, I'll just tell her there is an arsonist on the loose."

They both laughed as they headed to the parking lot to start their day.

* * *

After a morning briefing, shortly after I came into the investigation, Daley and I were sitting at the conference table having one of our talks about the case. There was an incident that he could not get out of his head and he was seeking my input to try and help ease his thoughts. The fire happened Wednesday, October 8, at 0414 hours, and Daley was sitting in his Explorer drinking a cup of coffee and trying to stay awake when the call came over the radio. It was a quiet, 55 degree night. He had been on patrol with other members of the Task Force, riding around in the Northeast part of DC. The incident seemed to haunt his mind.

"Bob, this night was crazy. It had been really quiet. There was a good amount of people out as it was a pleasant night but the radios were quiet. Everyone was bored to death."

"I hate those kinds of nights, I said. "Staying awake is a bitch. What made this call stand out to you so much?"

"DC was dispatched for a fire at 1315 Otis Street. We had people just blocks away and they arrived ahead of responding fire crews and saw smoke and flames on the front porch. The arsonist had to see them. Firefighters arrived, and our people asked them to just darken the flames but try to really not disturb anything."

"How did that go over? I don't think you mentioned that the last time we talked about this. DC isn't much on people telling them what to do," I said.

"I know, but nobody said a thing. It was done without any backlash. Crews made quick work of the blaze and the bulk of the fire damage was only to the front porch. There was a heavy acrid smoke odor which permeated every part of the home. I have always wondered what was burning. All the evidence was collected and transported to the lab."

Tom continued, "The thing that gets me is we had people there really fast and they didn't see anything out of the ordinary. I can't figure out how the arsonist got away without being seen."

My reply was short. "I still don't have a solid answer for you just now but let me try this. Were there any good places he could hide and watch?"

"Hell yes, Fort Bunker Hill Park was directly across the street."

"How close was the Metro?" I asked.

"The Brookland Metro station is only a few blocks from there."

"Partner, I think we just answered your question of how he got away and wasn't seen by anyone. The guy hid in the park until he got his jollies watching the action and then he slipped off to the Metro."

"Great theory, but the Metro is not operating at 0400 hrs," Tom said.

"Thanks, way to screw up my great work. Maybe he had a car a few blocks away and just walked to that and left."

"Perhaps," was all Daley said.

* * *

It was clear to those present at Otis Street, the fire was the work of the DC Arsonist. The team experienced both exhilaration and frustration with being so close to catching someone in the act. Questions quickly came to every member's mind. *Is he, she, or they watching us? Where is he or they? Why this home?* A significant presence responded to the Otis Street area. Bystanders and vehicles were stopped, drivers licenses and tag numbers were recorded.

Another major law enforcement operation that revealed nothing.

Following the fire on Otis Street, the fires stopped for about a month. Media attention intensified. Arson stories were broadcast daily. The public information aspect of the Task Force was working hard to sooth the tattered nerves of an anxious community. Area fire chiefs were joined by both federal and local law enforcement leadership to present a united front at a press briefing and provide as much information as they could without compromising the investigative process. The arson investigation had become the major news story of the region. People everywhere were talking about the case. Everyone knew something or at least thought they did. Each news agency had a different piece of information but they were all pieces they should not have. It appeared that somebody was talking that should not be, and the investigators were pissed.

Sitting in the investigators office, Derek Chapman, a state fire marshal was talking to anyone who would listen. Chapman was a well-built African American who kept his head shaved bald.

He was president of the fire marshal's union and liked by just about everyone. He worked hard and could be counted upon when you needed something done.

"What in the world is going on? I cannot believe somebody is telling them our business," he said.

Everyone in the room was listening but nobody responded to his comments. They were wondering when the next shoe would drop.

It finally happened.

Bad news about the investigation was reported. One news agency ran a story on the ten o'clock news about the case. As with every criminal investigation, investigators try to keep a few key pieces of information to themselves. This is done not only to try and protect the case and the people who have been victims, but to prevent the suspect or suspects from knowing exactly what investigators know. The news began with viewers being teased by a reporter saying, "We are going to show you exactly what the arsonist is doing when setting a fire."

Members of the Task Force, sitting in their homes, watched the broadcast in disbelief. The story started with the reporter on location at one of the homes devastated by the arsonist. The reporter was standing on the front porch of the burned out home as he told viewers, "This is how he does it."

What he did next just simply blew everyone on the Task Force away. He held up a one gallon plastic milk jug with a yellow-looking substance inside. The reporter told viewers the arsonist took some type of cloth material like a sock, made a wick, then lit the wick. He actually held a lighter in his hand, placed the device, and walked away.

He actually did it!

The following week was a bit stressful for the Task Force. Some investigators wanted to arrest the news reporter; he had in fact made an incendiary device, right? Was the substance really gasoline?

Some wanted to summon him to appear before a grand jury and have him tell them where he got his information; others wanted to remove everyone on the Task Force and bring in new staff. A difficult and challenging case was made more difficult by the reporter's actions. Monday morning Derek was blistering mad and he was quick to let everyone know it.

"I want this guy brought in to be interviewed and I want him charged."

He slammed the table and shouted, "This guy has to be taught a lesson. He can't just broadcast this kind of stuff and nothing happens. We have to find out where the leak is and we need to find out now."

Fingers were pointing in every direction and, trust me, no person or agency was left untouched. In the end, no one person or agency was found to have provided information to anyone. There were several personnel transfers and many, right or wrong, thought they were a result of the information leak.

Chief Blackwell, fire chief in PG County, talked with several of the other fire chiefs the day after the news piece aired.

They were not happy. Chief Blackwell met with the news director of the television station and expressed his extreme disappointment. He did not go easy on the news director as his level of frustration was as high as the investigators. In expressing his disappointment, he shared the collective concern about potential copycat incidents.

The consequence of broadcasting the design of the device could have a very negative impact on the work the Task Force was doing. To the best of my knowledge the reporter was removed from covering the fires, but the damage was done.

There was no fire activity for thirty four days. Task Force members wondered if the person was lying low now in light of the news describing his actions in detail. The calls on the tip line did not slow down. Investigators were still dealing with the look-alike leads and working the night shifts. The daily briefings became more interesting as staff started to develop their own ideas on what was going on and who was doing it.

"Fulkerson, I think the arsonist is getting information from somebody that is on the Task Force," quipped Sam, a very outspoken DC detective.

"Sam, I can tell you that we are looking into that but nothing has turned up."

"Well it sure looks like he knows more about what we are doing than he should. I can't believe the guy is that smart."

Fulkerson's reply was a bit more direct this time. "Sam, do you have anything constructive to bring forward or do you just want to bitch."

"Scott, I'm just frustrated like a lot of these folks, but they won't say anything."

"Look everybody, I'm just as frustrated as any of you," said Scott, "but it's critical that all of us remain focused on the facts we know and not allow ourselves to be swayed by the many different opinions and theories that are out there."

Scott was trying to be a good leader but he felt outnumbered.

During one of the many briefings that lasted far beyond the intended thirty minutes, Folger suggested an idea that had everyone listening.

"Our suspect or suspects seem to be shopping mainly at local area convenience stores that are open late. If they are using these locations to purchase the jug, we need a way to identify which store the purchases are being made from," Folger said.

"I think we take a metal marking tool and scribe into the bottom

SOLVING FOR X

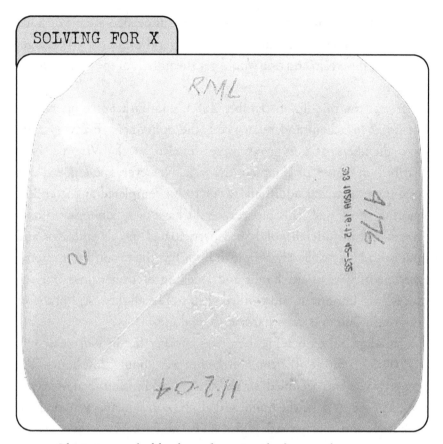

*Plastic jug marked by the author using the four quadrant system
to track stores the arsonist may have used to purchase materials.
(Image courtesy of the author)*

on the jugs some type of identifier. When we have a fire, we can have the lab look at the remaining plastic and ID the store of the purchase."

After a thorough discussion, those in the room had a few questions. "Does anyone think this would work?" Sam asked.

"Do you have a different idea?" replied Folger.

"Is there a single location we can go to and do this?" asked Daley.

It was decided they would try it. If this worked, it could make the case. A single location was identified in Virginia that serviced thirty-eight stores in the areas that had been impacted by fires set by the suspected arsonist. The bottom of the jugs could be divided into quadrants to be marked and not draw any unneeded attention. One area would get a store number, one would get the date, one would get the day of the week, and one would get the initials of the person doing the scribing.

It was the middle of October 2003, and Task Force operations expanded to accommodate marking the containers. Every evening three members of our group were detailed to the Virginia 7-11 distribution center to complete the task. Not everyone enjoyed this assignment as it was additional work to be completed at the end of a normal work day. This process would have to be done seven days a week and include all holidays. I participated in this endeavor and understood very well why people did not like the detail. I went home every night with sticky hands and smelling of fruit drink. But the process was important and worked well, so like all the rest, I just kept my mouth shut and did what had to be done.

Tuesday, November 11, there was another fire in Northeast DC at 1700 24th Street. The time of the fire was about 0230 hours. The property was an occupied single family dwelling. The device was placed in the front of the home and all the components were present, recovered, and transported to the ATF lab. Task Force investigators on the scene conducted a number of interviews. No new information was gathered, and again there was frustration as Task Force members arrived just after the first arriving fire unit.

The arsonist had gotten away again.

CHAPTER 5

Analysis

The National ATF Lab was utilized for all of our trace evidence reviews:

- 55 submissions to the lab
- 47 separate incidents
- 25 cases associated by physical evidence

The lab and the people who worked there were one of the most critical parts of our case. They dedicated a room in the lab just for our evidence.

The lab is actually two labs located in a sprawling industrial park in Ammendale, Maryland. The building is a secured, nondescript concrete structure, fenced and monitored by a federal security force; there was nothing indicating what type of work takes place there. When you go through the main entrance, you enter the Forensic Sciences Lab, one of three labs the agency has around the nation. Some of the best and brightest scientific minds work there. They conduct work in such areas as chemistry, forensic biology, document examination, fingerprints, firearms, explosives, tool marks, and engineering.

The main floor had classrooms used for continuing education classes for state, local, and federal officers. Additionally there were two large meeting rooms for conferences or other types of programs, and there was even a small museum. You could see examples of early cameras used, how pictures went from a single plate to black and white, to using chemicals and developing color images. I was in awe every time I visited. I made it a point to stop by the museum whenever time allowed. The remainder of the first floor is workrooms for experiments and testing. The second floor is made up of offices and small work spaces.

The next area you enter after going through a series of doors is the Fire Research Lab, most often referred to as the FRL. It was the only one of its kind in the country at the time and they have been doing great things since they opened in 2003. One of the coolest parts in the FRL is the Burn Room.

The FRL employs two full-time carpentry crews who are able to construct just about any type of building needed for burn simulation. These crews re-create a building that has been burned, thus allowing investigators to actually test a burn theory. If an investigator is going to say that a fire was caused by something, they have to be able to prove that theory. Conducting controlled burns allows the theory to be tested.

The largest smoke hood/fan I have ever seen in my life was in the Burn Room. The unit is able to ventilate out all the smoke and fumes in just a matter of minutes. The FRL video records all the work it does from multiple angles and heights, and makes the videotapes available to the investigators as they work in completing their analysis of the fire incident.

The staff conducts many different types of work such as flashover studies, fire pattern analysis, and the impact accelerants have on fire growth and spread. They conduct electrical fire cause analysis and many other fire-related tests. Another cool aspect of the Burn Room is the water system. There is a water cannon that can flood the entire room should a fire grow out of control. They also have a water recovery system that collects, cleans, and filters all the water used, getting it ready for the next event. In all the months of our investigation, going to the lab was—for me—the best field trip you could ever take.

The Task Force held meetings at the lab and had dealings with many of the sections and staff during our investigation, but we dealt with one primary scientist, Ray Kuk. He responded to fire scenes from home and always went above and beyond the call of duty to assist us. He was a guy that made science fun. He was friendly, always had a smile on his face, and always had a kind word, even at 0430 hours. He was one of smartest people I have ever had the pleasure of meeting and working with.

Ray had a knack of making the work fun. One time while in our evidence room, he helped me solve a problem. "Ray, I cannot figure out how you know what it is in each one of these piles of plastic. I understand you look at them under a microscope but how do you tell what is what."

Ray smiled and said, "Bob, look at each of these piles like a piece of lasagna. If you want to know how it was made, you have to take it apart layer by layer. Each layer reveals another thing that shows you how the lasagna was made. I take each one of these piles and peel back each layer and reveal another item. When I'm done I know what's in each pile."

The real bonus for the Task Force was having the lab so close to us. The lab took a single room and made it our evidence room. We could go to that room with Ray and look at each fire scene and see exactly what each piece of evidence was that was collected. Ray could put anything we wanted under a microscope for us to view, and he could provide us with a detailed analysis of anything we had recovered. We were able to see how one piece of evidence collected from one scene compared to a similar piece collected at another scene. It was fascinating to look at all those melted circular piles of plastic and look through them and see melted bag material or melted fabric. Truly, a one-of-a-kind education.

We had fifty-five submissions, and each address had their own table covered with butcher block paper so nothing dropped off or got lost. This may seem like no big deal, but believe me, when there is a single place to go and see each piece of evidence in your case, it's a big deal.

My experience with most cases, I had crime scene photos and photos of my evidence but that was about it. If investigators get really lucky, the lab they use isn't too far away and they can manage to get there once every couple weeks, and when they do get there, they might be able to see a single piece of evidence and that is about it. Our lab was so close we could visit daily and we had everything collected at our fingertips. Investigators and scientists at the lab always made themselves available and never said no. The Montgomery County crime lab did all of our DNA evidence examinations. We got reports back in just a couple weeks as opposed to a couple months. It was faster than anyone could ever imagine.

CHAPTER 6

Serial Arsonist
Profiles and Motives

Fire has a somewhat universal fascination. For most who ultimately become obsessed with fire, it starts as a youngster watching a campfire or a bonfire. This common behavior that soothes some becomes a destructive force in others. What concerned me throughout my entire fire investigation career was the community at large and the courts in general associate this crime as one of the least violent. It is most often looked at as a destruction of property and only in some rare cases will the court look at the state of mind of the fire setter. While most serial arsonists dissociate themselves from the damage they cause and the harm to human life that may result from their work, their crimes are not less violent and dangerous.

Arson is the deliberate act of setting a fire. In the law enforcement profession, crimes are classified by the seriousness of their nature, either a Part I or Part II crime. While arson is considered a Part I crime like murder, rape, and robbery, in most cases it is tracked separately. Setting a fire is one of the easiest crimes to commit and one of the most difficult to prove because people are able to do it under the cover of darkness and are seldom seen, and therefore there are very few witnesses.

Serial arson is the act of repetitive fire setting. This is not a motive or some type of diagnosis, it is simply a term used to describe the pattern of fire setting. For some reason people don't seem to fear the serial arsonist in the same way they fear the serial murderer.

In our case we did not get many calls on the tip line from people in Virginia until a fire was set there. I cannot understand that.

The Profile:

In recent years there has been a great deal of material written about the profile of a serial arsonist. Being an arsonist is different from being a serial arsonist. When I began doing fire investigations, the FBI and ATF placed the serial arsonist in one of two types: organized and disorganized. This really was way too generic, and today serial arsonists can fall into many different categories. This author believes serial arsonists are so unique that each one is different in their motives and often cross over into more than one category.

Ed Nordskog, retired LA sheriff fire investigator and serial arson profiler, suggests an easier to understand profile:

- 90% of serial arson fire setters are male. Mobility of the arsonist is often limited. Most do not drive or own a vehicle.

- Target selection on their first few fires involve targets they have a personal connection to or grudge against.

- They have a limited criminal history with no known arrests for arson.

- Their typical interaction with law enforcement is for theft or vandalism. If the serial arsonist does own a vehicle and can drive, they will usually drive very fast and very erratic.

As the Task Force team sat around the office one day, the discussion focused on serial arsonists we knew. Folger mentioned John Leonard Orr. "Maybe the most famous of them all."

My response was long. "He was the most famous to us because he was a fire marshal. He wanted to be a cop and tried to get on with LAPD but washed out after failing the psych exam, then he took the test for LAFD, somehow passed and got into recruit school but was washed out again because he could not meet the physical requirements. He ended up getting hired by the Glendale Fire Department in Glendale, California."

Folger kept it going, "He was a real cowboy, always in trouble for getting involved with all types of crimes outside his area of authority. He never thought any of his fellow firefighters or police officers were as good as he was."

"Hell, I think we both could say we have known one or two like that over the years," I said. "Would you not agree?"

"Bob, it has been way more than one or two, but Orr was a real piece of work," said Folger. "I read an article that estimated that in the ten-year span from 1980 to 1990, he may have been responsible for as many as two thousand fires. The article went on to say he would travel up and down the California coast going to training and setting fires all the time. He became one of the best-known investigators in the state, because he had a real knack for being able to pinpoint an exact point of origin when nobody else could and was always able to prove what he was talking about."

I was quiet for a minute as I thought about how hard finding an exact point of origin was. Nobody is that good. Finding the exact point every time.

"I just love the story about Orr feeling the need to write a novel on fire investigations. His ego must have been so big he had to duck walking through doorways. The best part is the book helped lead to his arrest," I said.

"What was it called again?" Folger asked.

"It was called *Points of Origin*." I said.

In the book he wrote about a commercial building fire where a young boy and his grandmother die. Interestingly enough there was a real life fire where this same thing took place.

In the book the young boy had the same first name as the boy who died and then he said in his book the boy had been eating an ice cream cone just before the fire started. In the real life incident the little boy had in fact been eating an ice cream cone. A fact that had not been published and would have only been known to someone who had been at the scene of the fire just before it started.

"Orr's balls were as big as his ego," said Folger.

That comment drew laughter from everybody who had been listening to the discussion. John Orr was the original Barney Fife. He was not physically fit compared to other firefighters. He liked to carry a large handgun, and seemed to get involved in bogus events like high speed chases and foot chases. He was an in-your-face cop to the homeless and juveniles. He had a knack of blowing every incident out of proportion. He was in fact a pretty poor investigator.

Orr had no criminal history, but was accused of minor theft and embezzlements on multiple occasions. He was a frequent drinker, serial cheater who was married four times, and there were some questions about his sexuality, which he never agreed with.

Orr may be the most famous serial arsonist that people know of because he was an arson investigator and fire marshal. He used devices to set his fires, was very mobile, and even used disguises. He was dangerous because of setting so many fires within occupied commercial structures. He was very sophisticated and both walked and drove to his targets. Orr was a thrill seeker, a firefighter, and a vanity and revenge arsonist. When Orr was arrested, he never admitted to his guilt and to this day denies any involvement.

Up to this point, we had been looking for someone setting fires

John Leonard Orr

- White Male

- Difficulty in Relationships

- Controlling Personality

- Wanted to be in law enforcement since childhood

- Heavy drinker

In the end, Orr's reign of terror produced:

- Five deaths

- Sixty-seven brush fires per year for ten years

- Millions of dollars in damage

in the early morning hours from 0200 to 0600 hours. We had been looking for someone setting fires at occupied locations, single-family, and multi-family dwellings. They seemed to like to visit locations or areas they knew and were familiar with, and they were using a device we had not seen before in the region. We were looking at the most common motives of arsonists to assist in helping us determine why he was operating in a particular way.

In 2016, the U.S. Fire Administration suggested a variety of arson motives.

> **Crime Concealment** - Set on purpose to cover up things like murder or burglary or to eliminate evidence left at a crime scene.

> **Excitement** - This motivation includes thrill seekers, attention and recognition seekers. Favorite targets include occupied structures, dumpsters, trash, and vacant houses.

> **Extremism** - Setting a fire to further social or political or religious causes. Extremist motivated targets include animal labs and abortion clinics.

> **Profit** - Offenders expect to profit from their fire setting either directly for monetary gain or more indirectly profit from a goal other than money. Targets range from personal property to commercial buildings to people.

> **Revenge** - Retaliation for some injustice, real or perceived, by the offender.

> **Vandalism** - Malicious or mischievous fire setting that results in property damage.

> **Serial Arsonist** - Someone who habitually and compulsively sets fires.

Based on the number of events, their frequency and locations, arson is classified by type as single, double, triple, mass, spree, or serial.

Single, Double, and Triple are all defined as a single fire set at either one, two, or three locations with no cooling off period for the arsonist.

Mass is defined as three or more fires set at the same time in the same location.

Spree is defined as three or more fires set at different locations, also with no cooling off period for the arsonist between.

Serial is defined as three or more fires set at different locations, with a period of time passing between them.

A true heavyweight in the serial arsonist world that lacked any type of sophistication is Paul Keller. With the exception of a retirement home fire, most of his fires were not very dangerous. He was a very mobile arsonist and his fire setting progressed as he worked the area. His motives included a bit of excitement and some vanity as he really enjoyed following his own exploits in the news.

Keller was an hyperactive child who had outbursts of anger and violence against his siblings. He grew up in a very loving home with a family that owned and operated an advertising firm. After some failed jobs he went to work in the family business and became a successful executive and salesman.

Keller became a fire buff very young and twice failed to become a firefighter, narrowly missing the cut.

In August of 1992, at the age of twenty-seven, Keller began his reign of terror which lasted six months. He targeted churches, nursing facilities, warehouses, businesses, and homes. In all, he was responsible for setting over one hundred fires. Most of his fires were set on the outside of structures using available materials to start them. He had

---

Paul Kenneth Keller

- White Male
- 27 years of age
- Loner
- Troublemaker
- Fascinated with Fire Service
- Alchoholic
- Trouble with relationships
- Never felt close to parents

In the end, this is what Keller's reign of terror produced:

- 100 fires in six months consisting of residential, commercial, warehouses, nursing facilities
- Killing of three
- Thirty-five million dollars in damage

---

no criminal history, led a stressful life that involved high-pressure sales, bankruptcy, and a failed marriage. He was a heavy drinker, smoked pot, and spent time with hookers.

In the end, it was his family who alerted the police and advised them they thought Paul was the serial arsonist they were looking for. When Keller was arrested, he confessed to the entire series of events and seemed proud of what he did. He became cooperative in assisting the investigators, even taking them back to many of the scenes.

CHAPTER 7
A Turning Point

Nvember 16, 2003, a cold Sunday morning, and the case took a major turn. The arsonist had set thirty-four fires that we knew of up to this point. Twenty-one of those fires had been set in Washington, DC, and thirteen had been set in Prince George's County, Maryland. At 0451 hours Alexandria was peaceful, with most of its residents sleeping deeply, in their two-story homes with two cars parked in the driveway and well manicured lawns. A city with a rich history, situated along the shores of the Potomac River, sitting just ten miles or so south of DC and about the same distance north of Mt.Vernon—the home of our first president, George Washington. It's diverse population of 159,428 residents composed of 21% African Americans, 16.1 % Hispanic Americans, and 60% White Americans. A city of just fifteen square miles.

A fire occurred at 4410 West Braddock Road. The structure that was set on fire was on the grounds of a nursing home called the Lynn House. To this point in the investigation, the Task Force had not been working with any agencies in Northern Virginia and none of the investigators from the surrounding areas knew what to look for. This fire seemed to meet some of the items, which had been released in the news. It was in the early morning hours, the home was occupied, the fire was near a door—but that was it. All the other locations which had been hit by fire were in mostly working-class neighborhoods and were directly next to either the Capital Beltway—an interstate highway that makes a complete circle around parts of Virginia, Maryland, and Washington, DC—or Route 295, also known as the

Baltimore-Washington Parkway. The Alexandria fire, while less than two miles from the Beltway, occurred in an affluent area.

As with any incident in Alexandria, I was contacted by my communications center and advised about the details. It was a little after five in the morning so I just stayed up. I went downstairs to our computer room and called the on-duty fire marshal. It had been a busy week and I had received early morning calls the past several days. I really didn't want to wake up anyone and hear complaints about all the early phone calls. I really wasn't thinking anything out of the ordinary at this point. I was just doing my regular follow up with staff.

"Good morning Russell, what do you have?" I asked.

"Well chief, I'm not really sure. It was an outside fire, directly next to the main entry door."

"OK, anything else?"

"The house was occupied by one person, no injuries and I'm smelling gasoline or some type of petroleum product in the air."

"Interesting. What's your gut telling you?"

"I think it may have been set. I still need to interview the occupant a second time and really dig the debris a bit more before I can tell you for sure."

"OK, Russell, do you need any additional resources?"

"I could use one more to help me."

"I'll call one of the daylight folks in early and I'll be there within the hour. Later buddy," I said and ended the call.

I headed to the shower, and while getting dressed, decided to hold off calling the boss until I knew a bit more. No sense ruining his last hour of good sleep. I was out the door, picked up coffee and was on the scene within forty-five minutes. When I arrived, there was a single engine still there with it's red lights flashing and I could only think how much that flashing hurt my eyes. I made a mental note to tell the crew they could turn their lights off.

As I was walking toward the scene, I saw a small single-story frame house.

The ground where it had been built was lower than street level and I had to walk down a few steps to get to the front. There was a diminutive split rail fence across the front with some bushes which helped block the view of the home from the roadway. I also noticed the home was directly across the street from a private school and city park, places that would provide easy concealment for someone not wanting to be seen at night.

Approaching the burned out area at the front door, I saw my investigator, Russell, with his beanie pulled down over his ears and looking like he needed a shave. I knew he needed the coffee I had picked up and suggested we take a break and enjoy the warmth of my buggy and the coffee. That brought a smile to my haggard man's face. As I walked to the car I was deep in thought.

Could this be the arsonist? In most extended arson investigations it isn't uncommon for the suspect to make some changes. Sometimes they need more of a challenge, sometimes they are afraid that where they have been setting fires is too full of investigators and they better move. Most of the time they just want a different target. There is no way this is connected.

After a short warm-up we continued to look over the scene and I decided to make a call to the Task Force and ask about what we should be looking for. Daley answered his phone on the second ring.

"Tom, it's Bob Luckett. We are on the scene of a residential fire and we think it could be the work of your arsonist. Can you tell me what we should be seeing or what we should be looking for?"

"At most of the fires we are finding a circular pile of plastic at or near a doorway," said Daley. "It is easy to miss and in many scenes this pile gets moved as part of the burn debris. When the area around the burn is looked at closer, an outline of a circular pattern can be seen. There is the odor of a petroleum product in the air and damage is normally localized to the fire area."

"Okay. Let us go look a little closer and I will call you back."

"Hey Bob, can you give me the address just in case so we can look it up now and have an idea of where we need to go if you need us?"

"No problem, it's 4410 West Braddock Road in the West End. One block from the Alexandria Hospital. Later, I'll let you know."

It did not take us long to find and see the things Daley had described. The circular pattern was on the porch landing by the door and the burnt plastic pile had in fact been shoveled into the burn debris.

"Daley, it's me again. We found the stuff you told us to look for and I think you should come take a look."

"Ok Bob, we are already on the road and will be there as quickly as traffic allows."

"Ok, wait, did you say you are already on your way?"

"Bob, you don't call me out of the blue unless you have a real good reason. As soon as you called me the first time I knew we would be needed. So I just started the team that way."

"Daley, you're a piece of work, buddy. See ya soon."

The evidence team along with a K-9 arrived in short order.

Once on the scene they needed only a few minutes to locate the device in the debris pile. All the components were present, and the dog "alerted," indicating a possible positive identification of a flammable liquid. It can only be a positive identification when a lab confirms the sample. Alexandria had now officially become a member of the Task Force, which would have to be called the Maryland, DC & Virginia Regional Arson Task Force. The City of Alexandria, Virginia would need to assign someone to the group. The logical choice would seem to be the investigator who caught the call.

The fire chief and the chief fire marshal had a meeting to discuss who would get the assignment. I got selected. I was never told why they chose me, but it was very cool to learn that I would be going. That feeling of total happiness left rather quickly when the boss dropped his little bomb. I could go to the Task Force and remain assigned as long as I returned to the office daily and kept up with all the open investigations and did my daily supervisory paperwork.

As the chief deputy, I was responsible for a staff of seventeen: nine investigators and eight inspectors. Each day I reviewed inspection results and fire investigation reports. I handled questions from business owners with concerns about code violations and met and talked with prosecutors on upcoming cases. A tough assignment, but I still wanted it very much and agreed. I was being given a chance to be part of an investigation that covered the entire region, an area of more than 1500 square miles. I was excited to meet and learn from what I hoped would be some of the best in the business. Perhaps I could contribute something that might help. I would have agreed to just about any plan if I could work on the case. Working on a very hard case excited me. I saw it as a challenge.

Over the next eighteen months my boss found a way to make the Task Force assignment work. On several occasions, to honor my commitment, my workday often began at three or four in the morning. I may not have gone in every day and most times when I did, it was just for an hour or two, but it worked. My boss covered for me more than anyone would expect.

This is a good point to discuss how one needs to keep superiors informed about sensitive case investigations when there is a mixture of sworn law enforcement people and non-sworn, non-law enforcement people in charge. My direct superior and the chief fire marshal for the Alexandria Fire Department, Mik Conner, could not have been any better. I was fortunate my supervisor was a sworn law enforcement officer. We had a tremendous respect for each other and he had a keen understanding of the Task Force's duties and the need to protect confidential and sensitive criminal information. I'm sure he at times was careful when explaining my whereabouts and hours to our bosses. I know he candy-coated things that went to people above us, but sometimes you have to.

The top boss in my office was not a law enforcement guy, even though he tried to make everyone believe he was. For the entire time I worked under him, he always tried to pressure me into providing him the juicy details of any investigation my staff was involved in. This is a

SOLVING FOR X

4410 West Braddock Road, Alexandria, Virginia
(Images courtesy of the author's files)

very touchy subject, as this type of person is the boss and they have to answer to someone as well. They never want to enter a meeting or be asked a question and not know the answer, but criminal investigation work is a totally different arena than dealing with non-legal matters.

I'm not boss bashing here, but trying to explain how it really is. Provide them the most basic version of the facts, telling them only what the public can know. Keeping the sensitive and confidential information to yourself is a must.

Administrators are just that, they administer the work; they are not investigators and while they often have to keep sensitive items quiet, they, for some reason, just cannot seem to do it with criminal matters.

*　　*　　*

Driving to his office alone Scott Fulkerson was thinking over many, many things.

This fire at 4410 West Braddock Road in Alexandria would now require additional changes within the Task Force. When the unit was formed it was agreed that any jurisdiction which suffered a fire would be offered a position within the administration. No one including me ever expected the arsonist to strike in other jurisdictions. He had been operating in DC and PG for months and getting away every time. There was no need to worry about any changes. What direction do we go now? The Virginia fire presented another issue which needed to be quickly addressed. Our arsonist is on the move. Where would the next fire take place? I need to get investigators from both fire and police the information on what to look for and how to contact the Task Force, and what our operational response would consist of if they need us. There is plenty of work to do.

The overnight shifts were eliminated as the number of leads had now reached almost 1000. We needed the staff to work leads full-time and bring those numbers down.

The September 11, 2001 attack exposed a need for improved communication and working relationships between police and fire departments of various jurisdictions. Frequent conversation with and exposure to our law enforcement partners had improved, but there was work to do. These agencies have been getting the job done together for as long as anyone can remember but they had not done it willingly very often. While the work that has been done many times was similar and on almost every call police and fire are together, they are different. Working together as one unit, sharing information, splitting command responsibilities, having a single presence all require a good bit of work.

CHAPTER 8

Changes

Fulkerson, Hoglander, Daley, T, and I—the supervisors on the Task Force—held a meeting to determine the best course to follow with assignments and duties for all the staff assigned. There had been so much talk all around the country about the need for agencies involved in any given incident to work under a single umbrella of command. We needed to find an approach that would work for everyone.

The fire service had been using the Incident Command System for many years. Prior to ICS, the fire service interaction with other government agencies were often disjointed. At large scale or complex incidents involving multiple agencies, communication was one of the biggest challenges. Use of ICS during our investigation was a valuable method of ensuring continuity, communication, and resolution of a difficult case. Working a fire scene in a location we had not been to before is a great example. The fire company did not know us and was a bit standoffish when we first arrived. The extinguishment of the fire was complete and folks were standing around waiting for fire investigators to complete their work. We were able to seamlessly get into that process by becoming just another branch of the investigation section. Our people worked alongside of the investigators already present and in about half the time were able to go through the debris pile and make the determination that the fire was not going to be part of our case.

The firefighters were happy because they were getting to leave sooner and the investigators were happy because they not only finished sooner they were also able to ask ATF to look at the evidence they collected just as an extra way of making sure the case was not ours. A win for everyone involved. One of the nice things about ICS is it allows you to use what you need when you need it and keep off to the side what you don't.

The Task Force was broken into three sections: administration, evidence, and investigations. Task Force staff would be assigned to one of these groups and report directly to the group's supervisor on a daily basis. The group supervisors, along with case agents, would make up the command staff. Two-way communication throughout our investigation made the Task Force work much easier. After the morning briefing, each day my group and I would go to our work space and talk over problems they were having with the leads they were working or ideas they felt were worth looking into. Anything that came out of these sessions that we felt would be helpful would be taken back and discussed with Daley and Fulkerson.

As the scale of the investigation grew, our work was unfairly impacting Prince George's County more than it should have. More staff and other investigative resources were being assigned. We had reached fifty officers working on a daily basis. We needed to get the information in more people's hands. We were also faced with the possibility of needing to call upon public safety agencies in all the locations at one time. Supervisors openly worried how would we do this? We knew timely sharing of information was vital. The Task Force had to face the challenge of getting information distributed widely in a quick and efficient manner.

Emergency communications centers in the region had a well-established mutual aide radio system that allowed look-outs, pursuits, and other important messages to be passed along seamlessly to multiple agencies.

The law enforcement community uses the Police Mutual Aide Radio System (PMARS) and the fire service uses the Fire Mutual Aide Radio System (FMARS). There is also the Amber Alert System which is a great way to communicate to a large geographic area or across the nation. After several long discussions, we considered the Amber Alert System to be the style of tool we needed.

Working with area fire and police chiefs we developed the Fire Alert System. Once the investigation was able to develop a suspect or suspect vehicle, we would be able to broadcast a look-out that would allow law enforcement and fire personnel to hear what we were looking for.

This information would then be provided to all units in service and operating on the street. Police cars, fire engines, medic units, fire marshals, detectives, etc. Every public safety officer in the region would know who or what we were looking for. If an agency had located what we were looking for, they would call the Task Force direct and we would respond to their location.

The process for sharing information across the region created yet another challenge that required direct contact presentations and briefing sheets: one for law enforcement and a second for the fire service. Portions of the information from the presentations was also used for interactions with media, neighborhoods, and other interested groups. We needed to make sure every agency in the three-state area knew what we had and what we were looking for. We developed two presentations. The one for law enforcement outlined the more in-depth particulars of what we knew but wanted to keep secure. The plastic bag for example. Almost all of the evidence collected and examined showed some type of plastic bag. The public did not know this and we didn't want to tell them. The second presentation for fire people and other non-law enforcement folks outlined what the general public knew but covered the details a little more in depth.

Once the briefing sheets were ready, we had to get the information out. We established a schedule to cover all the police and fire departments in the region.

Task Force members attended all the regional and state meetings dealing with fire investigations and provided them with the required information. We did one additional thing when we met with all these groups. We made a pledge to each:

If you have a fire and think it may be related to the serial arson case, call us. We will respond to your jurisdiction and look at it. If you make an arrest and think the person could be the serial arsonist, call us we will send someone to interview them. We do not care what time it is or the day of the week. If you call us someone will respond immediately to your request.

Among our many investigative initiatives, none was more important than getting information to public safety officers on the street. The men and women who patrol, respond to calls, and apprehend suspects bring new ideas and important information every day they are on duty. Keeping them informed was crucial. Maintaining the interest of all involved about our incidents and other activities over a twenty-two month period was daunting. We knew we could not be in every locality every minute. We knew that the best chance to catch an arsonist was to keep the information updated. The system worked well, and law enforcement and fire departments from the region did call the Task Force. We looked at scores of fire scenes that were not the work of our arsonist and we interviewed many folks that officers thought could be the guy or may know something about our case. None of these things alone would close our case but what it did was keep our case fresh in their minds. We were able to talk directly with many people who asked lots of great questions, and we hoped one of these calls would get us a break.

Pursuing a lead in the wee hours was part of the job, driving across the three impacted jurisdictions often in heavy traffic to examine a fire scene was at times frustrating and driving fifty miles out of the way to talk to some mental subject was seemingly outlandish, but it had to be done and without doing it we would have lost one of our most important resources. The men and women of public safety, who live each and every case together. With so many incidents taking place in the areas of DC, Maryland and Virginia if we did not do this, our case would just have been added to the growing pile of cases. By reaching out to them and then constantly following up with them, this case stayed in their line of sight all the time.

Investigators had an entirely new set of issues to review. They had been looking at fire crews in Maryland and DC, now they had to mix in the crews from the Virginia fire departments. Members of the unit began to examine potential persons of interest that worked or volunteered as firefighters. The region is transient in relation to where people worked and volunteered. Some firefighters worked in Virginia and volunteered in Maryland, and often work schedules differ. There were also considerations related to how close someone may live to the impacted neighborhoods. What Virginia firefighters, if any, were off on all the dates of the fires. What time did they leave or arrive at work? Conducting these searches took weeks to complete.

Drinking coffee one morning, Tom and I discussed this because I was convinced the arsonist was a firefighter.

"Daley, I still think this guy is a fireman. He came to Virginia and set one to throw the Task Force off."

"Okay, if you are right, where do you think this person works?"

"I'm not sure, but if I had to guess right now I would say either DC or PG."

"How do you propose to narrow our search down to one agency or the other?"

"Again, I'm not sure, but I figure to start by looking at fire crews who were off duty for all the fires."

"Bob, that was done early in the investigation and we didn't find any consistent numbers. In fact, no one crew was off for all the fires."

"You guys had to miss something. I'm telling you the arsonist is a firefighter."

"If you feel so strongly about this you need to do your research before you bring anything forward. If you don't, you'll just be throwing stuff at the wall to see if anything sticks. We have way too much going on to be chasing our tails anymore than we already are."

"Copy that, buddy. I'll work on it at home and see if I can come up with anything."

We began to receive many more leads on the tip line from Virginia callers. *What are we going to do?* The holidays were coming and the commanders felt there were some investigators who were not pulling their fair share of the load. It was difficult to tell if some staff were just dealing with boredom or if there were some other underlying factors. The simple fact was that when investigators had leads and were not following up to finish them, it created a problem. There were many discussions on how we should proceed. There were several choices: should we stay the current course, should we reduce the group and attempt to do more with less, or should we ask for additional staffing in hopes the fresh blood would help?

Every choice had pluses and minuses. In the end we decided to reduce the number of investigators assigned. Our hopes were to get the most interested people to stay and with that get the most production. The results of our decision with just a few exceptions, we got just that. Those who remained assigned to the investigation stayed the course and with their dedication and hard work closed the deal in the end. When there was a callout, everyone assigned responded to the scene. We were able to cover all the extra details and assignments were getting completed in a more timely manner. The Task Force was informed about what changes would take place and everyone that was not going to return was asked to complete their outstanding assignments before the Christmas holiday.

The rest of the month of November 2003 remained quiet. This allowed us to catch up on all outstanding leads, plan for the reduction in staffing, and set up the schedule for the new year, including the Christmas schedule. In fact, we decided we would operate with a skeleton crew for Christmas week and asked all investigators to just work from their own offices unless they were off, and to be available if there was a callout. A meeting was held with chiefs from all agencies involved and all of the planned changes were announced. We knew more fires were going to happen and we needed to be ready when they did.

The month of December came and we still had not had another fire. The weather was turning cold and the schools were ready to go on Christmas break. With all this going on, Scott had secured us a new work location. We would be moving to a very secluded and secured location at the Maryland Agriculture property. We would have total use of a four-story brick building. The plan was to move in by the first of the year when all the staff reductions had been completed and the holidays were behind us.

The Task Force met with an ATF personal profiler on Friday, December 19. Our profiler, Ron, was a veteran investigator with a strong background in crime scene analysis, crime scene recreation, working with witnesses, photographs, paths of travel to and from crime scenes, and crime scene notes. In preparation for our first visit, Ron revisited fire locations and neighborhoods during time periods the crimes were committed. During the meeting we outlined the information we had: fires were taking place between 0200 and 0600, and all the locations had been occupied. All fires had been at or near an entrance or exit. We asked for more detailed information and Ron shared the following analysis based on the information we had given him earlier: the person we were looking for should be under a great deal of stress right now since holidays bring on the stress, he more than likely has family or personal relationship issues, and he was likely African American based on the fact that most of the fires occurred in predominantly minority neighborhoods during times when he could move about and not attract attention.

"These issues will cause this person to offend again soon," the profiler said.

"If the arsonist does not set another fire in the next week, I will provide all the doughnuts for our next meeting."

The room broke into cheers and laughter.

*　　*　　*

On Saturday, December 20, 2003, at 0437 hours, we had another fire. It took place in Prince George's County at 5702 83rd Place, New Carrollton. The device was set at the front of the house near the garage door. The home was occupied at the time. What makes this fire more interesting was the fire location was about one mile from our Task Force command center. The fire occurred the day after our meeting with the profiler. Every element of the fire was consistent with the previous arsons. It was a "wow" moment that increased the Task Force faith in science. The profiler told us we were going to have a fire. It also caused some members of the Task Force to again wonder about potential leaks from inside the workplace. That frustration was apparent at our morning briefing the next day.

Derek started things. "How the hell does this person set a fire so close to our command center?"

"Scott, he makes a great point," I said. "Is someone that is part of our group talking outside?" My question brought additional comments.

"I was thinking that too," Sam said.

"It sure seems like he knows what we are doing," Derek said.

I continued with, "Did one of these people that just got moved out set a fire to laugh in our face? I hate having these feelings but I do. We need to catch this person and it needs to happen now."

Scott had listened quietly, but with my last comment he spoke, "Much of what you guys said I would agree with to some degree. Throwing out negative comments about our group or those who are no longer here really doesn't serve us well. I wish we could catch the person right now as well but it really doesn't seem practical at this very second. I think we would be better served if all of us took these built up frustrations and put them to work running down all our leads and developing something more useful."

The investigation of the New Carrollton incident continued for the next couple weeks. We had a plethora of photographs to review and interviews to follow up on. We found a boot print in the dirt near a hole in a fence one block from the scene. The fence separated a shopping center and the housing community. The area was not well lit and appeared to be a good place to park a vehicle and walk to the site of the fire unseen. We were excited when security video from a motel one block from the fire was collected. The videotape showed a vehicle on the roadway coming out of the housing community when the first arriving fire engine turned onto the same road. The vehicle turned their headlights off and allowed the fire engine to proceed. As the engine began turning in front of that vehicle, it flashed the headlights and then drove away, stopping at a traffic light. When the light changed the vehicle made a left turn and proceeded toward the Capital Beltway. Within ten minutes the same vehicle was seen returning to the parking lot of the motel and backing into a parking place. The vehicle appeared to be in a position to watch the street where the fire was. The vehicle did not stay more than a few minutes before leaving, and did not return.

The quality of the tape did not allow us to get a clear picture of the vehicle or the driver. The ATF surveillance technicians were called in and they worked until almost 2100 hours to improve the quality. All the work and effort that went into the tape yielded nothing. In the end all we knew was we had a car turning off their lights, then flashing their lights, leaving and returning to apparently watch the fire, and then leaving again.

Investigators were assigned to work with the still pictures made from the tape to narrow down possible vehicles. The following day investigators were back out looking at more video from the motel and reviewing registration logs. They found a tour bus leaving the lot just before our vehicle was seen. We found the bus company name and learned they had a small list of drivers. We reviewed trip logs and found nobody had a trip logged in. We continued to dig and found that a driver set up a trip on their own and did not log it. The driver was interviewed and he could not provide us with anything more than we already had. We quickly ruled the driver out as a suspect and we talked with the bus company owners and tried to make it okay for him.

This was the final fire for 2003. Our New Year's Resolution was to catch the arsonist as quick as possible. The Task Force held its first Christmas party and the year ended quietly. During the holiday season the three brothers from the incident on Anacostia Avenue were re-interviewed and got their first look at the Maryland State Police sketch. Reggie said, "It looks stupid," and repeated those words many times. Ricky, his brother, said simply, "It looks like some sort of robot drawing. Using this won't catch anyone." The third brother didn't say anything, he just shook his head.

Undeterred, the Task Force explored the practical use of using the services of a sketch artist to create a more lifelike pictorial. Our discussion was shared with prosecutors, assistant attorneys general, and assistant state's attorneys that may be called upon to prosecute.

Many did not believe it was a good idea. However, there was a conscious decision to not involve all three brothers in the sketch process. The attorneys were then a bit more supportive because there would be one, that in their minds, was not tainted by the process. We continued to discuss it and made the decision that the artist would not talk to all three of the boys.

CHAPTER 9
Look-Alikes

Thursday, January 22, 2004, at 0311 hours, there was another incident. This marked additional changes in the work of our arsonist. The fire was not set at a single-family residence. The fire was set in an occupied multifamily dwelling. I was sleeping good for a change when the phone started ringing. I yelled "hello" when I picked it up and questioned the fact that I was being told it was an apartment building on fire.

"Can this be correct? An apartment building is a big change."

Fulkerson, the Task Force boss said, "Yes, it's an apartment building, now get your ass moving and we will discuss the particulars later."

It was very cold and just two days after our first snow of the year, and I had to sit while my vehicle warmed up. Another call out in the middle of the night. I scraped the front and rear windows quickly with my handy fit-in-your-hand window scraper and waited for the warm up. As I watched my breath in the cold air, I had the same first thought I always had: *Please don't let there be anyone who has lost their life and please no injuries to anyone.* I don't know why this was always my first thought but I can't change who I am. I had a co-worker tell me that it was a reminder of why I got into the public safety profession. I wanted to help people so this was my way of keeping that fresh in my mind.

Snow still lay on the ground and along the sides of the road. There was a frozen crust under my wheels as I drove along and the sound of that was all I could hear. I turned on my lights and siren to drown out the crunching noise. This fire was just a mile from the command post, in the opposite direction from the fire on December 20. It made us all wonder again if the arsonist was toying with us or trying to send us some type of veiled message.

When I arrived, all I could see were bright lights. The press was everywhere and my eyes hurt. There were a lot of people standing around in night clothes who looked really cold and they had a haze of the smoke floating in the air around them, mixing with exhaust smoke from running vehicles. The snow that fell was now pushed into mounds to make the parking lot driveable. The mounds of snow had covered several parking spaces and vehicles were parked haphazardly all over the place. The parking lot looked like some type of maze. I took a moment before I exited my vehicle and thought about what might lay ahead for my team. There were going to be a massive amount of interviews to conduct. I had also noticed on my drive that there were several business locations that sold gasoline and they were open. Investigators would need to visit each one and check on small gas purchases and video. I knew this was going to be a very long day.

The fire was set in a common stairwell between the lower level and the ground floor. All the parts of our device were present. The placement was interesting: though placed on the stairwell, it did not prevent the people living above from exiting the location and did not prevent those living below from exiting because there was a door on the lower floor. There was thick black smoke in both directions but the fire was off to the side. *Why would he do it this way?* What was of bigger concern here was his move to an apartment building. Had he become bored with single-family homes? The people who lived there didn't really care, all they knew was someone had set their building on fire and forced them out into the snow and cold.

As I approached the command post there was an ongoing conversation amongst the commanders about buses being requested to get the displaced residents out of the weather. I quickly added my two cents and said that whatever the final number they were requesting to please add one more for my team to use for interviews. Interviews at an incident scene were never fun because people have been pushed out of their home. Adding the snow and cold only made them worse. They usually went one of a couple ways: "Mr. and Mrs. citizen, I'm investigator Luckett and I need to ask you a few questions. Will that be okay?" The response: "Is it going to get me back into my home any faster?" Then there are always a few like this: "I'm investigator Luckett and I need to ask you a few questions about what happened here tonight." The response: "Are you stupid? There was a fire in my building and now I'm out here freezing my ass off."

Investigators would spend most of that morning in the buses and the next week locating and interviewing everyone in this particular building and talking to the residents in the buildings around it. Nothing new was found. Our arsonist had stepped it up a notch by moving to an apartment complex and not one person could offer us anything positive.

I was hoping he would become a ghost for a while. We were preparing a major presentation for all the area chiefs and I wanted time to work on my part uninterrupted. I'm not downplaying the importance of working the case here. Educating the top officials in the area was a key element needed to be able to gain resources and keep all our staff currently assigned. Building a quality program takes time and we were stretched really thin already.

Friday, February 6, at 1100 hours, we arrived at the ATF lab to make our big presentation. The weather was horrible; it started out snowing in the early morning, then changed to sleet about noon, forcing area schools to close early and add to the growing gridlock.

Driving in snow or bad weather in the DC area is infamous. Snow is not removed like it is in the north and for some reason just an inch of snow can shut the entire region down. Nothing moves. It could mean nobody would be at our meeting and after all this work I would be pissed. We prepared a good bit of information for this so we sure didn't want it to be for nothing. Hoglander and Daley were busting each other's balls about how much work we had done and the fact we have this thing all set up and nobody was there. I called my boss to make sure he was coming and he told me to be patient. "It's snowing," he said.

Things started out a little late, but the room was filling up and I wondered if the work we had done would be enough to impress the importance of the case. The room was full of many VIPs: DC Police Chief Charles Ramsey and a couple of his commanders, Prince George's County police and fire chiefs, and a few commanders from each of those departments: Chief Fire Marshal Mike Conner from Alexandria and the Maryland State Fire Marshal. In total more than twenty-five people attended as participants and they asked really good questions. Did we have enough staff? What could they do to assist us? It would appear we were on the right track. As we left for the day we felt good about what we had done and where we would go.

In just a few weeks we would be flying in Lois Gibson, a sketch artist from the Houston, Texas, police department to make a new drawing. Gibson had helped law enforcement identify over 750 criminals. While our legal staff was not keen on the idea, we decided we needed to try anything that could help in catching this person. The artist would speak to all three brothers and decide which one she would use to develop the new drawing.

I headed home feeling pretty good and made arrangements to take my wife out for a good meal. We were at dinner with friends when at approximately 1700 hours, I received a phone call from a fire investigator with the Fairfax County, Virginia fire department. There had been a fire in an apartment building near Route One. He asked if I could come out and take a look at his scene because he thought this could be the work of an arsonist.

"If it was 1700 hours now, what time was the fire?" I asked.

"The fire was reported at 1456 hours at the Cherry Arms Apartment complex, 7701 Richmond Highway," he replied.

It was the middle of the afternoon. Kids were home from school because of the weather. This seemed unusual. The fire had been set at a front door to a lower level apartment and was blocking a stairwell door. *I knew this could not be our guy.* I told the Fairfax investigator I would be there as quickly as I could.

I returned to the table and told my wife and other dinner guests that I was needed at the White House. "It's urgent," I explained with a smirk, "they need to talk to Cupid with Valentine's Day rapidly approaching and they need some expert assistance." I offered my apologies to the other couple and asked them to take my bride home.

Not happy at all, my bride kissed me and said, "Be careful."

I drove as quickly as I could to Cherry Arms Apartments. After arriving and reviewing both the fire scene and evidence collected by the fire investigator, I knew I had been wrong with my thought that it could not be our guy. I was confident this fire was the work of our arsonist.

The arsonist added another twist to the pattern. This fire was in the middle of the day with many people at home, and again nobody saw anything. The setup of these buildings was quite interesting as well; enter in one building and travel on the bottom floor and exit four buildings later. This type of design made it easy for our guy to have parked two blocks away at an elementary school, walk in unseen, place the device, set the fire, and leave unseen.

The pattern change concerned me. If the urge to set fire was so strong that he was setting them in the daylight the potential for loss was going to mount quickly. I called the other commanders and told them I found another device or something similar. There was a plastic circular item with what appeared to be a plastic bag of some sort and it was all melted into a pile near a door. There was no need to activate the Task Force as all the initial scene work had been done by Fairfax investigators. We could return on Monday and begin our canvass based on what Fairfax had not already completed.

This fire yielded all our device components and the bottom of the jug provided a UPC code which allowed us to determine the product was a jug of Classic Selection Spring Water, sold at grocery and convenience stores throughout the region, including 7-11 and Giant Food, a large food store chain in the region. Marking the bottom of jugs was as important as ever.

On Monday morning, staff from Fairfax County Fire and Rescue attended their first Task Force briefing. The Cherry Arms fire which I had responded to on Friday was discussed in detail. Everyone was buzzing about what appeared to be an emboldened arsonist acting in a brazen manner by setting a fire during broad daylight. It certainly made members of the staff wonder what was going on. We had two fires set within a mile or so of our command center and now one was set just hours after our meeting with officials from all the regions in the area. More puzzling was how this most recent fire was set and not one person interviewed could provide anything useful. The resident manager's office was just a few doors away from the unit where the device was placed. People were in and out all day long and again not one person reported seeing anything unusual.

The week would be very stressful as all staff began to look at the last three incidents for any possible connections. They checked on vehicles that had been seen in the area for a match of any vehicle seen at the other incidents. The results yielded nothing. The weekend would bring a welcomed rest.

Thursday night dinner at my home was going to be lasagna and my wife and I were going to plan our day for Saturday. That was Valentine's Day and we were going to discuss the events of the day.

When I walked through the door I was met with a wonderful aroma of garlic and knew my dinner was in the oven.

"Honey, I'm home."

"I'm so glad you made it home on time. Dinner will be ready in fifteen minutes," my wife said.

"Just enough time to throw on my sweats. Will you please pour me a glass of wine?" I asked.

"That's already done, just go change."

When I sat at the table, now very comfortable in my sweats, my wife put a large slice of lasagna in front me, I began to laugh. My laughter did not go over well at all.

"You haven't even taken a bite and you're laughing. I know you do most of the cooking around here but how about giving me a chance," she said.

Shaking my head and putting up my hands in defense I said, "No you got it all wrong. I'm not laughing at your cooking at all. At the lab the other day I was working with one of the scientists trying to understand how he came up with results when he was looking at a pile of what you and I would say was nothing. He told me it was like going through the layers of lasagna. Each layer revealed a different ingredient and when you finished going through the layers you knew what you had. When you put my slice in front of me his explanation came flooding back."

"You are so full of shit it's not funny," she said.

"Honey, I swear that's the truth and now each time you eat lasagna you'll be laughing too."

Our meal was great and we made plans to go out for a steak dinner on Valentines' Day.

*　　*　　*

On February 14, 2004, at about 0510 hours, the phone rang. I picked the one up by my bed and got a dial tone; my wife elbowed me and said, "It's the other phone and you left that one in the family room."

I hurried downstairs and caught it on the fourth ring. There had been a fire at 7700 Blair Road, Silver Spring, Maryland, the first fire in Montgomery County. The Task Force was activated by the command post.

When the Task Force is activated, someone at the command post pages everyone and then contacts all the supervisors, who in turn follow up the initial page with a phone call to all the investigators on their team.

This process normally involved calls being placed to about fifty people each time. I thought about telling my wife it was the White House again, needing more help from Cupid, but knew it would not play well. I kissed her and said, "I'll be back soon."

I was on the road but not sure of the location; the Nextel phone was working overtime and in just a few minutes I contacted my entire group and they knew we were going to another new area, one that had no fires before. When I finally arrived on the scene, I learned the fire call came in at 0456 hours, and the first arriving units found people hanging out the windows on the upper floors, screaming for help from this four-story walk-up garden-style apartment building.

The first few minutes were chaotic for all the firefighters, as they had to effect multiple rescues from both the interior and the exterior. They were also met with multiple injuries as some residents had exited the building on their own and had to go through the flames to get out. There were two burn victims, a teenage female, and a tiny female child less than 10 years old. When units arrived, firefighters and paramedics were able to treat the injured, get the girls transported to the hospital, and extinguish the bulk of the fire.

The scene was more under control now and members of the evidence team found the device had been placed on the stairwell leading from the first floor to the second. The evidence team began to do the dig. Digging a fire scene is a process where investigators go through the debris looking for evidence: collecting, preserving, and packaging it. During this process, they found a large piece of black material that looked like a pair of man's pants. Our last fire, at Cherry Arms apartments in Fairfax, Virginia, had material that looked like black pants. Were they the same?

As in all fire investigations, assignments were made to interview every occupant who was still at the scene. Investigators were sent to the hospital to interview those victims. A canvass team was sent into the community to visit retail gasoline locations, look for small gasoline sales, and obtain video surveillance. Prior to everyone heading out on their assignments, we reviewed what we knew. We learned that the front of this location was in Montgomery County, Maryland, and the street directly in the rear, was part of DC. Did our arsonist know where he was or was he trying to throw us off somehow? The building was a set of three and they were set up just like Cherry Arms; you can enter from one and go along the basement into the others and exit from any of the three. There were no security locks working on the doors, so entry was easy.

We spent almost twelve hours on the scene and Valentine's Day was out the door. All I wanted was a hot shower and a bed. I had called my wife, Caryn, many times throughout the day, trying to keep her in the loop in hopes of having that Valentine's Day steak dinner, but we both knew it was not going to happen; in fact, that hot shower and bed was going to have to wait just a bit longer as well. It was going to be a long weekend.

Sunday, February 15, Daley and Fulkerson headed out early to pick the artist up from the airport.

"Scott, do you think this lady is worth the money spent to bring her here?"

"I have thought about that over the last few days and I came to the following conclusion. None of the three brothers like the sketch that we have now. The lady has been helping Houston PD for more than a few years and they seem to be pleased with her work. At the end of the day I don't think we have anything to lose."

"I'm fascinated with this kind of stuff and I cannot wait to see what she comes up with. My wife and I have been talking about it all week," Daley said.

They took her to her motel and then out to the command post to meet with the three brothers. After speaking with each one individually, she selected the one who would assist her in developing the new drawing and the others were thanked for coming in. After just a few hours we had a new picture of our guy.

Scott and Tom were amazed at how different this new drawing

looked but understood the work was just the results of what one person had remembered.

Monday's briefing was another long morning as we now had to bring in yet another jurisdiction, Montgomery County, Maryland, and plan for our news conference. Each new jurisdiction that had a fire was invited to join the Task Force. Originally the plan was to invite any new jurisdiction coming on board to join and become part of administration, but along the way it was decided the unit would be better served with less supervisors and more workers. We were happy to have the additional assistance Montgomery County would provide.

In a span of eight days the arsonist had struck twice and elevated the danger to the community as fires were being set in multi-family apartment buildings. Now supervisors had to decide how we would cover such a large area that seemed to be growing weekly. Our list of leads had grown to more than 1200, our list of possible suspects to well over 200, and we were no closer today at solving the case then we were when the investigation began.

With the reduced number of investigators, things had improved greatly, but with so many new leads we were worried we would fall behind again. With the move to our new facility we had an idea of creating a War Room. This room would hold vital information about all the fires. We knew that when the new photo went out our phones were going to ring off the hook.

I had a conversation with one of the Maryland State Fire Marshals. Derek was a guy I had developed a good working relationship with and I trusted that he had a feel for how the rest of the investigators in my group felt about things.

"Derek, how is everyone feeling about all this work coming at them?"

"Bob, most of the folks knew it was going to be a greater challenge working with less staff but they were excited to get started because they wanted to see this thing to the end and catch the person responsible. Everyone seems ready for the challenge," he said.

February ended and March began like a lamb with no fire activity.

I received a call at my office from an apartment complex manager in Alexandria. When I called her back she told me the arsonist had been seen on her property. I went to the location alone before going home and interviewed every staff member who thought they had seen our guy. While I was driving there, I was thinking about why this guy would be in this apartment complex. *Was he looking to rent a place or was he scouting it to set another fire?* My mind was working overtime to try and figure out what this person was doing. He was seen on two different occasions by three different people. I took this information back to the Task Force and we decided to conduct surveillance of the complex for the next few weeks. The manager provided us with a vacant apartment and a local motel, directly across the street from the apartment complex, provided us with a suite. Contact was made with the Virginia Division of Motor Vehicles office located next to the apartment complex. They agreed to place some surveillance cameras in locations we selected.

A few days later, discussing the details of the set up in a morning briefing, people were eager to get the Alexandria gig. They did not have to sit in their car long hours overnight, but had a motel room or an apartment. Brian Padgett, a PG detective, yelled from the back of the room, "I'll take this detail faster than a witch getting a new broom."

Boy, this was a change. Brian did not volunteer for anything.

"Rotating watches, a bed or carpeting to nap on, a newspaper, and bathrooms. I would stand in line to work this, plus it's overtime," he said.

I worked the detail three times and quickly understood why Brian would want to work it: a great chance to catch whoever was setting these fires, get that overtime money, and be warm and not out in the elements all night. We watched the complex for almost a month until Saint Patrick's Day. Like many surveillance details, we sat, watched, and waited but whoever it was never returned.

A tip line caller provided information on a person who seemed to be out trying to impress women. They said he was telling people he was a fire investigator and this guy looked like the sketch we just put out in the news. The tip was discussed at our morning briefing but it was not until a day later that it got more attention. There was a report in the news of a person entering an elementary school in Prince George's County, Maryland posing as a fire marshal. This seems a bit too coincidental. Two folks posing as fire marshals did not make sense. One trying to impress the ladies and the other going into a school. Schools were not known as great places to try and impress the lady teachers. Task Force members were sent to the school to investigate and they notified the command center with the information they had. The suspect looked very much like our sketch. They were able to identify a vehicle, a white Volvo, and from that we got a name and possible address. With this information in hand we made the decision to conduct surveillance.

We staked out the Auburn Manor Apartments in Prince George's County, and on March 30, investigators saw our suspect loading boxes into the Volvo. They approached the suspect, and while talking to him, saw a Prince George's County fire department coat in the trunk.

The suspect provided investigators with a name and told them he was employed by the Fairfax County fire department.

The vehicle tags were run and found to be stolen; the suspect was arrested for being in possession of those tags. The suspect was then transported to a lock-up facility in Prince George's County for processing and interview. We had been planning for this since I became a Task Force member. We had someone in custody, we had selected folks to do the interviews, and we had people to check out any information gained during the interview. Everyone who needed to be in the command center running things and making sure everything got done was gone. They were either dealing with interviewing this guy or running down something associated with his arrest. Nobody was where they needed to be and it took way too long to accomplish everything we needed to do.

The day was long and those of us involved worked very late into the night. When sitting in a command post with several other investigators and everything that had been planned for and discussed for weeks seemed to be turning to shit, it is total frustration. I can't speak for the others but I felt helpless. There were things I knew that were not being done and I could not get them completed. Where was the criminal history of this guy that we ran a couple days prior? Who was taking charge of getting the vehicle towed and where was it going to be towed to? Who was responsible for seeing that every detail of the day was checked off? Tempers were short and some feelings got stepped on. There was some yelling and cussing, papers were lying all over the place, and the looks on people's faces was more of confusion than the looks of a well-oiled professional team. Somehow all the work got done in the end.

Throughout the day and night, my phone was ringing off the hook. I was getting a bunch of congratulatory phone calls for catching this guy. I thanked everyone but told them I could not be one hundred percent sure yet, we still had a lot to do, to rule him in or out. When I finally melted into a chair just after 2300 hours, I caught the end of a news broadcast that had the picture of the guy we had arrested and showed the second drawing we did in February. They really looked alike.

The next morning at our briefing, Daley was not present, as he and detective Brian Padgett were the ones on the Task Force selected to go to the jail in PG and pick the guy up for his court hearing. Brian was a detective who loved what he did. He worked as many off duty overtime details as he did regular hours. He was an imposing figure of a man standing well over six feet tall, shaved head and weighed an easy 220 pounds. Both his brother and father were in law enforcement. Truly someone who was married to the work they did. Padgett walked to the beat of another drummer and we often kept him well away when brass were coming to visit. We did not want him saying something to them that would get any of us in trouble. I told him a few times that as long as we kept him on his medicine things were fine. He would just laugh and twist his head in a funny fashion and tell me he knew it. He always seemed to find trouble—every office has a person similar to this. No matter what they did, someone saw it as being incorrect or out of place. The way I saw things, there was no person on our investigation team that would not take Brian into battle with them. He was a relentless investigator and in some ways like a bloodhound. Once he had your scent he was unstoppable. Once he was locked in, forget about it. You were going to jail.

One day, Scott gave Padgett an assignment and told him he needed to go into DC and look for a particular person. The person was a potential witness to a fire incident. This meant he had to go to St. Elizabeth's, the psychiatric hospital for the region. He was gone and had not been seen for about two days; when he finally called in and got Scott on the phone. Scott told him how worried we all were. We thought they might have locked him up.

Padgett said, "I have some fantastic news." Now Scott, being all about business, quickly told all of us to shut up. We gathered around the phone because we were at a point where we needed some positive news. Scott put Padgett on speaker so all of us could hear what the news was. He told Scott the good news, "I just saved money by getting Geico car insurance!"

This sarcastic response was just perfect. The words that came next from Fulkerson are not printable. Everyone in the room but Fulkerson was roaring and rolling on the floor. Padgett was able to get the interview but it did not yield anything useful.

Padgett and Daley picked up the suspect from the PG jail and were transporting him to the federal court house for his hearing. Daley just stared at the guy and was just totally blown away at how much he looked like our drawing. Before Daley went into court he had called us several times to inform us of this fact.

Our guy was being seen in federal court for lying to a federal agent conducting a criminal investigation.

Scott had one of Daley's calls on the speaker, "You guys know that I never stray from telling you that we have to follow the evidence and if we do, it will solve for X. If we stay with the evidence long enough and not allow ourselves to get side-tracked by all the other things that hopped down the bunny trail, we would catch the guy."

On this day Daley thought the evidence was the match of the picture to the guy sitting next to him. This veteran agent was not the only one fooled. The news media really ran with this story. They did as much background on this guy as we did. In the end they were wrong too, as a physical match would not be enough to move forward.

The suspect we had arrested was a career criminal and he was involved in a lot of stuff, but he had not been setting fires. The guy was violent and was a sexual deviant—he once choked a female until she went unconscious—but we could not find any fire setting in his background. We spent about six hours talking and interviewing him after his court appearance. While being interviewed, his true identity was found and he was charged with lying to federal agents. He did not work for the fire department and never had. He had friends who were volunteers with PG and he had taken some of their fire gear. We also learned that this guy had outstanding warrants in Virginia involving the Division of Motor Vehicles.

After things settled down, I returned to the apartment complex that we had staked out and showed them a picture of the man we arrested. Two out of three who had stated they had seen our guy were able to confirm him as the man they had seen.

We learned a couple of valuable lessons with this arrest. The plan we had developed for arresting and interviewing a suspect went down in flames. The people who had been assigned the interview allowed themselves to become involved in other aspects of the arrest and were not available to do the interview. We failed ourselves by leaving very few in the command center to make decisions and to stay abreast of what was going on. Commanders went to the scene of the arrest instead of staying put and commanding the event. We did not have all the people we needed to do the interviews and chase all the paper and reports we needed and the day never seemed to end. Investigators and administrators have to stay focused and never lose sight of what is going on. We were so driven to get those things done directly in front of us we forgot about the big picture. We could not focus on what didn't happen, but had to plan better and keep working for whatever lay ahead.

The next few days were spent reviewing all the plans we already had in place and identified why they failed. Next we made back-up plans so they would be ready if our original plans failed again. No matter how long someone stays involved in investigations, know that at some point whatever can go wrong will go wrong and there must always be a plan B and C and D just in case and staff need to know that those back up plans are ready when they are needed.

This all sounds elementary but if you don't put it in writing it does not happen. One person cannot be expected to know everything.

The month of March had come and gone and we had no more fires. We spent the best part of April investigating our fire marshal impersonator. We served several search warrants and logged many hours on the road. One rainy Thursday afternoon, we planned to serve a search warrant on a small farm near the Bowie, Maryland, racetrack where our impersonator suspect worked and lived in the recent past. There would be nine investigators from the Task Force along with four local Prince George's County police officers involved in serving the warrant. Prior to leaving our command center, we reviewed the operations plan. This took about an hour and presented me with a great time to remind everyone involved in ever having to serve a search warrant to read and learn.

One can never take for granted that just because someone is trained as a law enforcement officer that they know how to do things the way you think they should or that they do them the way your agency does them. In fact, most of the time, investigators learn that every agency will have a different idea of how something is going to be done and if they do not take the time to cover each detail down to who is riding in what car and which way each person is supposed to go then something can and will go wrong. This is called good communication and often gets lost in the shuffle of doing too many other things.

While I sat in a small cramped room at a police station and listened to an ATF agent cover their use-of-force policy, I found myself thinking, *how many local fire marshals ever cover their use-of-force policy before serving a search warrant, or even how many have ever been out on a search warrant or have a use of force policy.* I was thankful that I had been through some very difficult training and had been exposed to similar situations in the past that had prepared me for what I was about to do.

Many people would think a search warrant is pretty simple and low risk and most of the time they are correct, but we must always prepare for the times when it is not simple and not easy, and it should be done the same way each and every time.

Our search warrant was going to be served in an attempt to locate anything that could tie our fire marshal impersonator to our case. Newspaper clippings, websites we might find on a computer, pictures he might have taken at fire scenes, fire gear, or even documents that may have been indications about locations to burn.

We met in a shopping center about a half-mile away from the target. Everyone was in their vests and assorted gear. Everyone got in their assigned vehicles and off we went. As we neared the site, it was easy to see that all the vehicles we had would not fit in the small single lane road. People had to park further back and run up to keep up.

We jumped out with everyone going to their assigned locations just like we talked and planned for, but the unexpected happened. There were dogs and we couldn't tell if they were running loose on the farm. Someone needed to address that.

Luckily we had people who were trained correctly and with good communication skills. Scott reassigned one officer to check it out and the dogs were found to be chained. We were able to gather all the people on the farm into one location, conduct interviews, and search what we needed with the precision of a group who had been working together for many years. Had it not been for the fact that we spent the time to cover every detail, we may not have had such a good outcome. There is no such thing as being too careful. Later that evening when all the work was done and we were just in a BS session, this seemingly minor event involving dogs creeped into our conversation.

"Man, everyone was holding their breath when we approached the house and saw and heard the dogs," I said.

Fulkerson simply said, "Planning and communication. You must always have a back-up plan and when the time comes don't be afraid to use it. The officer I reassigned to handle that, had been told should we face some unforeseen obstacle, she would be used to correct it. When I called upon her to check the dogs, she simply went and did it and our operational plan never changed."

*   *   *

April 16, 2003 was a chilly 42-degree morning and the arsonist could no longer stand the fact he hadn't been setting fires. When he drove around, his mind was always working overtime. *My firemen really must need me. I haven't been very good to them and I'm sure they would like something to do. If I can find the right place, we will have some fun. I will let the red monster out, they can fight the monster and I can watch.*

It had been sixty-two days since he set his last fire and again he found himself riding the streets in a Oxon Hill Community in Prince George's County. The fire took place at 0329 hours at a townhouse located at 2401 Rosecroft Village Circle East, next to the Capital Beltway about two miles from Virginia. There had been one other break lasting over sixty days, and when the arsonist returned, he set his fire in Oxon Hill as well.

I asked Daley, "Does he live in this area? Did he grow up in this area? What is his connection, if any, to this area?"

"All the questions we will have to answer," Tom said. "I have some of the same questions and by day's end let's hope we have the answers."

With his twenty years doing fire investigations, Tom never allowed the complexity of the situation to cause him to lose his focus. Everyone always saw his red hair before the rest of him and he may have on crazy-looking or mismatched clothes, but he never lost focus. I loved working alongside him because watching him work was pure magic. He was a superhero when he was looking at a fire scene.

This fire involved an end unit townhouse and was set on the right side of the home next to the porch. During the evidence recovery stage, investigators located a receipt from a local Giant Food store in DC. On the receipt there was an advertisement for a local tax prep firm. We sent agents to the store in hopes of locating a video tape of our purchase. Too late! They had already re-recorded the tapes for the day we needed.

We installed our own cameras in the Giant, thus adding yet another store that we had to go to after every fire to gather tapes.

All the pieces of our device were present. This was a pretty unique townhouse community because there is only one way in and one way out. The press was on the scene quickly and it seemed as soon as an investigator talked to someone, so did a reporter. Many times this caused us to be working against each other, when in fact we both wanted the same thing: the bad guy arrested.

Three people occupied the home: the homeowner, her mother, and a female child. The mother was interviewed by the press and she called the arsonist "a coward" and "a son-of-a-bitch" in the interview. We spent all day interviewing residents of the community. Many people told us about seeing someone run from the home and a car leaving the area. We checked all the 24-hour locations, but none had security cameras that were working. We found a gas can stored in the bushes near one of the homes. We did not dare send investigators over to recover it, as the press would have been down on us like locusts. We set up surveillance on the gas can until the press left and we could recover it without incident. Just prior to the evening news we made contact with the homeowner and found they stored the gas can in the bushes to prevent the smell from coming into the home. We called it a day.

Because the arsonist returned to this Oxon Hill community after such long breaks, we decided to put up pole cameras so we could obtain video of cars entering and leaving the area. The camera would be a live feed and we would have to conduct regular checks on the tape. Pole cameras provide real time video at the location they are viewing. We kept between four and six cameras running throughout the investigation. Someone would visit the location where the monitors were, view the footage, and save anything that they felt was valuable. Whenever we had a fire, a federal agent was sent to review the tapes and collect what was needed.

When we had interviewed the townhouse owner we discovered she had been befriended by a male subject who we then investigated rather extensively. We found he had been working to bilk her out of money for the purchase of a vehicle. We checked this person out further and found he had a criminal record for narcotics and had done this same type of thing to women before. As we began to take a closer look at him, the homeowner received a threat letter in the mail. The letter said they "have done it once" and next time they will harm her kids and ended by calling her a bitch. There was a return address and name on the front of the envelope. We immediately took the letter and envelope to the lab for DNA and fingerprint testing. Agents were sent to the address on the envelope and found the man whose name was listed. They conducted an interview and quickly determined that he was not capable of sending the letter.

Though in his thirties, his mind was that of a 10 year old. He lived alone and had been in the neighborhood for many years. We made a check of his everyday life and found it to be pretty routine and easy for someone to track. There was a local liquor store where he cashed his checks and he was picked up by a private bus on the same days each week and dropped off at a work center. We started a file on the liquor store, work center, and bus service.

After weeks of checking everyone out involved with the Rosecroft Village fire, we were able to rule out all of the companies we had found listed on the receipts and their employees. We were now looking at everyone in the building where the guy listed on the threat letter envelope lived. We found a lady who lived across the hall from him who ran a small greeting card business out of her home. We also learned that this lady worked for the advertising firm who did the ad work on the receipt we found in the evidence at the fire. We opened a file on her. In a morning briefing Scott reminded everyone, "Just because the three brothers at the Anacostia incident saw a man, it did not mean that a female could not be involved and that is why each and every person who comes to our attention, male or female, white or black must be handled in the same way."

Padgett made the following suggestion, "Fulkerson, you should handle all leads dealing with females since you feel they need the same attention."

Scott replied, "Thanks Brian, but you have to take the good leads with the possible bad ones. If I told you that you would get overtime for every female lead you followed up on, I bet you wouldn't mind."

"Copy that," Padgett said.

In the end we were able to rule this lady out as being involved in our case or this particular fire, but we never found who was responsible for the threat letter.

After the Rosecroft Village fire, I decided I would ride around in PG County and try to gain a better feel for the kinds of neighborhoods we were seeing our fires in. The county is gigantic covering 500 square miles and has a population of about 865,000. It is one of the most affluent African American majority counties in the entire country, made up of about 62% African Americans, 27% White Americans, and 11% other nationalities. The county has a pretty high crime rate, accounting for nearly 20% of all murders statewide from 1985 to

2006. The areas where we were having fires all seemed to be working class areas. As I drove around I was seeing smaller homes but you could tell the owners were trying to keep the lawns manicured and bushes trimmed. There would be several that looked like this on every street, but I also was seeing homes with cars parked in the yard with parts lying on the ground, kids toys lying all over the place, trash containers overflowing, and the homes needing improved upkeep. Wherever I drove I saw people out, kids playing in the street, and small groups of adults either standing or sitting and talking. If our arsonist was African American, he could move about easily and nobody would be the wiser.

Our arsonist had changed how he operated; there had been fires at multi-family dwellings, there had been a fire in the middle of the day, there had been a fire on a holiday, and after taking a sixty-two day break from setting fires, he returned to a familiar neighborhood to set the next fire. We needed a miracle and we needed it quickly.

CHAPTER 10

Closing In

Daley had been communicating on a regular basis with an agent from the Seattle field office. Dean had been the case agent in charge of the Paul Keller case, and Tom had told him many things that we discussed like the kinds of places being set on fire and that the investigation involved more than a hundred investigators. The problems they had and how they handled them.

The Task Force met with Dean while he was in DC for training. We talked for about six hours and during this time he told us that after looking at our set up and operation he felt we were doing more than his Task Force did. He felt we were on the correct path, just needed to remain focused and stay the course.

Scott asked Dean a very good question. "The arsonist had returned to the same community after taking long breaks from setting fires. Was there some importance to this?"

"Keller did the same thing, so if we were seeing that then we should follow up on it. Serial arsonists many times follow the same profiles as sex offenders and may even have sex offenses in their background," Dean said.

"We haven't been checking sex offender files but we will get started with that tomorrow," I said.

"Your arsonist will have a type of infirmity, crooked teeth, strange scar, bad hand or finger, something will be odd about him. Look folks, while you don't know it now, when you catch this guy you will find you were on the right track all the time," he said.

What Dean gave us more than anything was the assurance that we were doing the right things. While it seemed very dark because we did not have a real suspect and were still having fires, we would catch him. This was a major shot in the arm and the next day when we relayed this information in the morning briefing, everyone's spirit was lifted. There was a renewed feeling of success, however small, and we really needed it. Finally something positive had come our way. For weeks our briefings were the same: fires, fires, and more fires, and each time, no new useful evidence was being gathered. I cannot express enough how important it was to have talked with and relied on someone who had been through what we were going through.

With the new information about how arsonists seem to follow many of the same traits as sex offenders, investigators began to search all the sex crime files. We went to all the local fire departments and asked them to review their files and see if they had any names of kids who may have been juvenile fire setters in the 1960s. We contacted local animal rescues and asked for names of people who may be known to them for setting animals on fire. We were working with all the local police departments to look for people who had arrests for sex crimes and also had fire setting in their background. After a few days we had several new suspects.

Another investigator and myself conducted an interview of a guy who was in the Alexandria jail on rape charges. This guy looked like our sketch because of a white patch in his hair and he was about the right age. He told us that setting fires was not his style and we are able to determine that he was locked up during some of our fires. Unless he was working with someone, he was not our guy. As we walked back to the car I had a thought, *Hunting for the DC serial arsonist is not always fun.*

We interviewed some officials from one of the local school districts about a former employee who looked like the sketch and had been known to be involved in a fire incident. It was not clear what his involvement was at the time, but it warranted further investigation. We checked with the Prince William County fire department where this guy was supposed to live and were able to find the file and get a look at the fire report that he was involved in. We conducted our normal background checks, consisting of a criminal history check, and a review with all area fire and police departments to see if they have had any contact with the subject. We looked at any criminal history we could find, checked real estate files, wage earning reports and DMV files. We interviewed the suspect and found it was not our guy. He was an initial suspect in the fire but the investigation showed he did not set the fire and was not in the area when the fire took place. He was just a friend of the person who was involved. This is how it went for about three weeks. There were several people who looked good when we got the initial information, but once we checked them out further they were cleared.

We had an investigator who went through the entire sex offender files in PG County, and he found a guy whose picture looked just like our sketch. The date was May 29 when the file was found, and we did the initial review. Everyone felt like this guy had a chance of being our arsonist. He lived very near our Oxon Hill community in PG County; he had been arrested for a sex crime involving an intellectually disabled girl. We couldn't account for all of his time during our fires. We decided to put him under surveillance. The first night, he led the team to many of the areas where we had been having fires. He was driving like he knew he was being followed and then got on the highway leading investigators toward Richmond, Virginia. The team was called off at 0300 hours.

In a morning briefing, we decided since our target was traveling to many of the same areas we were having fires and at all hours of the night, we should put a GPS tracking device on his car. We did not have enough solid facts to tie the target to our case at the time, and knew we couldn't get a court order, so we opted for a tracker, which is placed under the car and runs on batteries. A "bird-dog device" does not require a court order because it is just a temporary device not tied to the engine of the vehicle.

For the next five months, we used a team of six to seven people every seven days to go to this complex or to the suspect's work location to change the tracking device's batteries. There was one person assigned to get under the car and change the batteries, while everyone else was the cover team, making sure the changer was not seen or hurt. This event always took place between 0300 and 0400 hours and only lasted about an hour.

What the hell do we do for the next four hours until roll call? I wondered aloud in my car driving back home.

My wife, Caryn, questioned me about this. "Honey, why are you leaving the house every few days and sometimes are back within an hour or two? Are you seeing another woman or what?"

"Caryn, I don't think sitting in a car with my gun between my legs covering a guy who is crawling under a car to change the batteries in a tracker is anywhere close to meeting a girlfriend. Interesting? Yes. The same? No."

We continued to follow and track this individual until September 15. It took until then to actually confirm he could not have been at all our fires, and when we conducted an interview with him—which lasted about four hours—he provided us with everything we needed to rule him out. It was time to move on to someone else.

It had been twenty-seven days since our last fire. We were working the overnight shift and covering locations in DC and Maryland, but there wasn't enough staff to cover them all. I was riding with Marc, a federal agent from Maryland.

He started in the federal system as an inspector, checking out locations that handled firearms and explosives, then moved up to become an agent. He was assigned to the Baltimore field office and had been part of the investigation for a few months.

The guy was liked by everyone. He was a tall, dark, handsome guy with Hollywood looks. Always playing jokes and laughing. Nobody ever seemed to get mad at him and he had that clever way of never having the finger pointed at him when something happened. Little did most people know that when some prank took place, Marc had his hand in it.

On this particular night we were partnered up and in an area of PG County that had not seen much fire activity, but was a prime working class neighborhood.

"I've got a great location for us to sit and watch the area from," Marc told me.

Being from Virgina and not knowing anything about PG County, I told him, "Whatever you think is best is fine with me."

After a short ride around the inner loop of the Beltway, he took an exit into an area full of houses with a scattering of small mom-and-pop business locations mixed in. He pulled into the parking lot of what appeared to be an abandoned firehouse.

"Bob, this fire company could not pay its bills on time and money was disappearing. Chief Blackwell began to question where the money was going and investigated. When it was completed, the department was closed down."

"Marc, you always seem to find the humor in every situation," I commented.

"Bob, I try," came his response.

As we sat there, I thought to myself, *somehow Marc thinks this was a great joke. We were conducting surveillance on fires being set, and we were sitting in the parking lot of an abandoned fire company.* I just loved it. We set up next to the building where we could see the road but not be seen by any passing vehicles. We both had coffee and were ready for anything.

"Since we can't see behind us too well, it might be a good idea if you sit with your gun between your legs in case we get surprised," Marc said.

My comeback was just, "Okay then!"

It was about 0200 hours and we heard four or five gunshots so close that we should have been able to see everything, but we saw nothing. We started up the vehicle and began to look for the shooting scene. Nothing. We heard no sirens, and couldn't find an incident.

We were able to locate a cruiser in the rear of a building well off the road. We pulled up, ID ourselves, and told the officer what we experienced.

The officer spoke up and said, "No disrespect guys. Gunshots go off frequently. If someone gets shot, someone will call. That is kind of why you found me here. We are just so busy answering calls for service, if we spent our time on routine patrol being proactive we would not have enough units to respond to calls."

We said we understood and for him to stay safe and then drove off. "Marc, you have given me a very enjoyable night. Remind me to never ride with you again."

Marc just laughed.

Looking at my watch I saw it was 0430 hours so I started calling cars in so everyone could debrief on the night's activities before heading for home. Other than the gun shots, we had a quiet night. My cell phone rang and it was Barry, the investigator from Fairfax assigned to the Task Force. He had just been called and informed there was a fire down off of Route 1 and they thought it was our arsonist's work. Route 1 is an area directly next to the Capital Beltway, Route 495, and is also the first exit in Virginia after crossing the Woodrow Wilson Bridge coming from Prince George's County. The area was a mix of residential and commercial locations undergoing real change. It used to be predominantly white, and now had a mix of African American and Hispanics. I called all the cars and notified the other commanders to respond.

We got to 3403 Beechcraft Drive, a single-family home about three blocks from the Cherry Arms Apartments. It was a balmy sixty-eight degrees and I knew sleep was a long way off. The device had been placed on the front left side of the house. A neighbor across the street, leaving for work, saw the flames, and alerted the residents to get out. All the pieces of our device were present and we found footprints in the rear of the home near a creek. Fairfax County Police brought in tracking dogs but found nothing.

We spent the next few nights like we did after every fire, sitting in the area watching all the movements to see if the arsonist returned to look at his handy work. We returned the following week on the same day as our fire and stopped everyone. We asked them what they saw the night of our fire, showed them the sketch, and asked if they had seen or knew anyone who looked like this. We ran lots of tags but it was the same as always—we got the paper delivery people and people going to work.

Between May 13 and August 30, the Task Force had no physical evidence linking the serial arsonist to any fires in the area. We were called out a few times during this seventy-six day period to look at some scenes, but none were ours. This brought about the same old questions. Is the arsonist in jail? Is he dead? Does he have a job related to schools? Is he a college student who leaves the area during the summer? We begin to pull new people into our possible suspect list and check them out but as each one is checked, each one was eliminated.

I left for work each morning between 0530 and 0600 hours, just in case the traffic was bad on the one-hour ride I had to the Task Force command center. Monday, August 30, 2004 as I was gathering the last minute items I needed for the day and heading out, my pager went off. I checked it and found a note from my communications center about a possible fire in Fairfax County that sounded like it could be our guy. I hit the road and called in.

Every fire department in the region was aware of the arsonist. They all had been talked to and all the departments who had people involved knew the importance of keeping an eye out. I have to give credit to a communications supervisor who, upon dispatching one of the Alexandria units to assist on a reported fire on a front porch at 4000 Elmwood Drive in Fairfax County, thought he should inform me.

"Mike, this is Luckett. Thanks for the page, what do they have?"

"Chief, the call went out as a possible house fire. When the first unit marked on the scene, they said they saw fire on the front porch. When I heard that I paged you."

"Ok, that's good. I'm headed that way. Thanks again."

The call was just a few miles from my home and I was on the scene quickly. An engine crew was still picking up the hose used to extinguish the fire and the only other people on the scene was a media van. They were listening to the radio as well and responded to the fire. I circled the block just to see what was going on and placed a call to the other commanders to let them know what I knew so far. There had been a fire on the front porch of a single family home. The home backed up to the Capital Beltway and the Woodrow Wilson bridge was less than a mile away. There were no reported injuries and I had not had a chance to get a look at the scene and would wait for the Fairfax investigators to get on the scene before I approached it. I suggested holding off on the callout until I got a good look. When I returned, a county investigator was on scene. I identified myself and asked to just take a quick look. He agreed but asked that I didn't touch anything until his boss arrived. I took one look and knew it was our arsonist—I saw the device. I made the call and everyone from the Task Force responded.

The neighborhood was very similar to that of the Beechcraft fire which was also in Fairfax County back in May. There were woods in the rear, a creek to the side, the home was the last on the block, and there was green space nearby, as well as homes under construction. The device was left on the front porch and the time of alarm was 0544 hours. All the components were found and we knew we would be spending another long day in Virginia.

Fairfax County, Virginia is one of the richest counties in the country with a population of a little over 1,000,000 and covering about 400 square miles. It is known for its many high-rise business locations and expensive homes.

The resident of the home left for work at 0500 hours and a neighbor across the street was getting ready to go to work and saw the flames and called it in. He did not see anything unusual but did note that his dog was in the yard and was barking shortly before he found the fire. This neighbor, along with his teenage son, ran across the street to see if they could help get anybody home out of the house. The area this home was in was not well lit and it would be easy for someone to walk in unnoticed, set a fire, and leave. The street the home was on had many routes to leave by. Someone could have even parked on the shoulder of the highway, walked in, and walked out unseen.

It's an awful feeling knowing when you begin to think like a criminal. When I reached a scene I began to think about what the person who was responsible was thinking. Where did they park? How did they leave? Could they be seen? How were they carrying the device to make it look normal? I had to allow my mind to become like that of the people I was looking for. If I didn't think like they did, I could never begin to formulate plans on what they may do next, how they may try to do it, and more importantly, what mistakes they made.

We returned to the area the next night for our usual surveillance practices: stopping cars out at the same time as when the fire occurred, talking to anyone we saw out late walking, writing down tag numbers, and doing background checks. Over the next several weeks, we talked to many people. What we learned was what we normally learned—nothing. We determined that our guy had very little time to set the fire and leave, as the paper delivery people were at the home around 0530 hours, so the window of opportunity was less than fifteen minutes. Either he had been watching the area and knew what was going on, lived in the area, was very lucky, or simply did not care about being caught.

When hunting a criminal, investigators have to cover the area in which they committed the crime, and ask questions?

- Who was out at the time the crime was committed?
- Why are they there?
- What did they see, hear, smell or notice?
- How many locations have lights on?
- Do these locations have lights on every night?

- If they do, you have to go and talk to the residents and see what they can tell you.

- How many vehicles are parked in the area?

- Are they always the same or are there more vehicles on some days than others?

This is all part of the idea of thinking from the perspective of the criminal. You are trying to learn anything you can about how they move about. You are looking for any possible link to the crimes you have already had. It's boring work but it has to be done.

We always went back the next night and just watched the area. We then went back on the same night a week later and stopped everything that moved. We got car information, name and address information, and work information. We never got any positive hits related to our case. We locked up a few folks who had outstanding warrants for misdemeanor crimes or made some good case information on open cases for other departments, and this was a good feeling. We may not have been able to catch our bad guy, but we were taking some criminals off the street, and in the end, that is what our job was all about.

What we did was use proven and time-tested investigation tactics and use them the same way every time. We had to hope that sooner or later the information we collected would help solve our case. Each and every time you conduct an investigation you must do it the same and keep doing it until your case is over. Seasoned investigators who are willing to do it the right way are what will make the investigation successful.

I can recall one night after a fire when it was freezing cold.

My midnight briefing was a midnight bitch session.

"Ok folks we are going back to the neighborhood and will gather as much information as we can," I said.

"Luckett, this is bullshit! We stand out in the street stopping everything in sight and never get anything," Larry said.

"Larry, we have made several cases and locked up a few. It's something we have to do."

"That's a company man's answer and you know it. It's cold as shit and standing out there is useless."

"Look, I will agree that going back to these places after every fire is a pain in the ass but we have to do it. The first time we don't do something, or somebody directly related with the case will slip through the cracks," I responded. "I'll buy the coffee. Now let's get moving."

Don't misunderstand the fact that investigators are going to bitch and complain about going back into some community a week later when it is below freezing out and just stand around and stop cars and ask people questions about something that took place a week ago. They would rather be home asleep or chasing a lead they feel is worthy. They are going to let you know what they think. They may say it is silly and not worth the time and they will be using far more colorful language when they are telling you. But, if they care about the case and want to arrest the bad guy, they will do it and do it the way it needs to be done. It must be a team effort and having everyone involved willing to do the little things, will help solve the case.

CHAPTER 11
Harry Potter

September 8, 2004, nine days after our last fire, we had another. It was a rainy Wednesday morning, and while most of the Task Force members had not arrived at the command center for the morning briefing, we received a call from the DC fire department. There had been a car fire at 2800 Channing Street, Northeast, and the investigator thought it was the work of our arsonist. There had been a couple of residential fires in this area that were part of our case but no vehicle fires. Knowing we had no cars set on fire by our arsonist, it was decided that we would just send someone from the evidence team and one commander to take a look at what they had. Within an hour we got the dreaded news: it appeared our arsonist had now begun targeting vehicles. There simply was no way we could muster the resources and staff to look at vehicle and structure fires in three states. If we were going to remain consistent with our operational plan we had to make some type of change.

When investigators arrived on the scene, just across from the Metro Bus barn on Bladensburg Road, they found a vehicle parked in front of a home in a residential area that had a device placed behind the driver's side front wheel. We must have had some luck on our side. DC fire does not, as a matter of routine, investigate vehicle fires. With so many vehicle fires in DC, they normally will not respond unless there is a known suspect or some special information about the incident. This particular morning, an investigator was sent on the call, but we never knew why. He spent some extra time looking at this scene because he knew there had been some arson fires in the area and found what he thought was a device. A melted circular pile of plastic that had what appeared to be a plastic bag attached to it. Our arsonist was consistent if he was nothing else.

It was determined at the scene that the jug was a Deer Park water jug and the bag was from a 7-11. The day was spent interviewing the owner of the vehicle and we discovered he had a very interesting past and was involved with many different women. This could be the reason the vehicle was set on fire, as he was married.

We also learned that he was a Metro Bus driver. Like we did with every potential suspect, he was interviewed. Investigators looked at everything they could get ahold of: finances, marriage, social life, and job. The neighborhood canvass did not provide much information other than the vehicle was parked at around 0600 hours and the fire was called in at 0635 hours. Our arsonist had not only begun to target vehicles, he was setting fires in the daylight and did not seem to care if anyone saw him. Was the carelessness in his actions a sign that he was wanting to get caught, or a sign that his urge to set fire was getting so much stronger he could not control himself?

The overnight crews were now responding not only to house fires started on the exterior, but were also responding to auto fires. In Prince George's County, there are nearly a thousand auto fires per year, and DC has just as many.

We decided we had to refocus on the facts of the Anacostia incident involving the three brothers and try to gain additional information. Each of the three was brought in and interviewed by members of the interview team. This allowed us to gain more experience interviewing people connected to the case and it also provided us with a chance to get firsthand information from the brothers. I was not part of the team when the brothers were initially interviewed and really wanted to size them up for myself. I found them to be typical young guys, not worried too much about the world outside of what was directly in front of them.

They seemed like they wanted to help any way they could and tried to answer every question with more than just one or two words.

Each one was brought into the command center at separate times and interviewed. Each interview lasted about an hour and we were able to get better information on the type of vehicle they saw leaving the area.

With the assistance of the Montgomery County Police Department we developed a manual of auto types. This manual became a mugshot book just for cars. Now each time we interviewed someone who provided information about a car, we could have them look at the car book and pick out what they thought it looked like. The information provided to us by the boys indicated the vehicle was an older model vehicle, perhaps mid-1970s to early 80s. We were unable to get a make of the vehicle but the brothers said the color was either blue or green. Not great information but something is always better than nothing.

We decided to begin looking in the Oxen Hill community, where the arsonist had returned to after taking long breaks, and in Southeast DC for a vehicle that matched these types. We would run DMV information for the types of vehicles in the years we wanted, and then would send investigators out to photograph the vehicle and attempt to interview the owners.

How in the hell will we address the staff needs to get this done?

We had a discussion about staff.

"Does anybody have any ideas," Scott asked.

"Perhaps we could find more staff from the agencies that were involved to staff the command center and free up a couple more investigators." Tijuana suggested.

"We could ask about people assigned to restricted or light duty," I added.

"That could work. I'll look into it." Scott continued, "I'd like to get back to scribing the bottom of jugs again. This time I want to concentrate on just seven stores and send someone to each store and they will scribe in the store. The stores will be the six 7-11 stores we have identified and the one Giant Food."

"Where the hell are we getting the people to do this?" I asked. "Our folks don't have much left in the tank."

"We can ask the SAC for more agents. I know it's a long shot but all she can do is say no," Daley said.

"My last idea is to add more people on the street to try and cover the growing fire types we are responding to. I will just add this to my request to Theresa. I will schedule a meeting as quickly as I can," Scott replied.

We had a meeting with Theresa, the SAC from the Baltimore ATF office and outlined the ideas and asked that we be allowed to run them for forty-five days and see what they get us. We asked that a request for agents from outside the region be placed, and from that request we would fill the needs of our three initiatives which were scribing bottoms of jugs, looking at particular vehicles in the Oxen Hill Community, and adding staff to night work to cover the auto fires. It did not take a great deal to convince Theresa; she knew we were stretched thin and that if we were going to have our best chance of catching the arsonist, it had to be done. The request was made and we got six more agents from around the East Coast.

It was also decided that six additional agents would be pulled from Baltimore and DC, three from each office to handle the scribing program. These six would be allowed to schedule their own store visits but it must be done each day before noon. Once they had done the scribing, they could resume their normal work duties. With so many new faces and people who had no case history or knowledge of the area, we split our forces to mingle with the new investigators. This allowed the current investigator to bring the new one up to speed and provided someone with knowledge of how to get around in the area. I had some concerns about this because we had people already assigned to the case who still did not know where to go or how to get there. They would have to call and ask each and every time or if not show up late. I really knew nothing about traveling in DC and Prince George's County when the investigation began and I grew up in the area, although it was in Virginia. When I first got involved in the investigation, I had to call Hoglander from PG on every Maryland fire and ask how to get there. He was starting to get annoyed that I called him on every fire, so I purchased a map book and by the end I knew it pretty well. Believe me, the map book I bought was well broken in by the time we made the arrest.

There were a few who never cared enough to get a map book or even ask how to get places. In fact, in my eighteen months of going to fires in the middle of the night, these few never made it to the scene. They would make the briefings afterward, but just simply did not care enough to come out to a scene. They worked leads but for the most part did all their interviews over the phone.

They were assigned to the Task Force but they were never part of the Task Force. What they failed to fully understand was they were making it more difficult for their fellow investigators. A flat tire is flat wherever it is sitting. When someone is selected to work in this type of setting you have to select someone that is going to represent your agency well.

The night work continued to drain away everyone's energy, but we had to keep going. We could be close to solving this problem. Yes, there were times I voiced my displeasure that people were not coming out to scenes, but it did not change the fact that there was work to be done and people were looking to us to get it completed. There were many conversations with everyone about the importance of staying focused on the evidence we had at hand, and allowing the evidence to direct where we went. This was not as easy as it sounds. We all had our own ideas and wanted Scott to look at them as being the most important. It was essential to allow everyone to express what he or she was thinking, but we had to remain realistic. Keeping focused was a difficult task. If someone had an idea on the case, they could not just come in and present it and leave it at that. They had to also provide the ways to investigate the idea so it would bear some fruit. If there was no logical way to do that then the idea had no merit and we could not spend time talking about it. Luckily I would talk to Daley about my thoughts and he would always bring me back to the place I needed to be: focused on the evidence we had and expanding that into ways we could use to catch the guy.

Keeping everyone working together was not easy. Somehow we

managed to always get back on track as a unit. With my years in the fire service, I learned that solving the problems of the world was always settled at or around the kitchen table. Law enforcement folks don't have this luxury as they eat most of their meals out and often alone. Fire service folks eat at least one meal a day together. I took this knowledge and brought it to light whenever I felt we were getting a little out of focus or off track. I would prepare a typical Sunday morning breakfast for the Task Force. Firehouse Sunday morning meals are legendary. Depending on who you ask, our Task Force breakfasts are now legendary as well. I would stop on my way in and pick up all the grub and then slip away to our kitchen and start to work. Before too long, folks would follow their noses and find me.

"Man, Luckett, I could smell that bacon all the way down the hall," Billy quipped.

"Well keep your paws off until I'm done!"

"Come on man, just one piece."

"Folger, get the hell out my kitchen, before I smack you with my frying pan. I need about fifteen more minutes."

We had eggs, bacon, scrapple, hash browns, ham, biscuits, toast, sausage, pancakes, coffee, juice, and milk. By the time everyone finished, all the issues we faced had been solved and we were ready to go. Most wanted a nap, but we were all on the same page again.

When I started on the Task Force I had a good amount of experience in investigations. I had been told over the years that I knew how to talk to people and maybe more importantly, knew how to listen to them. I was pretty good at solving the puzzles involved with fire investigations. I knew we could get this case solved in sixty days or less. and told everyone that my first day.

With all that I thought I already knew, it did not take long for me to really find out how much I had to learn. Being part of an investigation of this size and importance really humbled me. I could not get enough of it and it completely consumed me. I never stopped thinking about it and even today I still have many thoughts about it. I had dreams about how we would catch the person responsible. I was always doing research on the computer looking for things we might try in our case investigation. I never truly understood how people retired from service and took an unsolved case with them. All the time it eats away at them to the point they cannot get beyond it. How many investigators have lost a marriage because of it? How many have gone to the bottle to find answers? I know now how it takes a person over, how someone becomes addicted to the case. I told many of the folks in the Task Force that I only wished I could have been part of this type of investigation in my younger years. To be exposed to something like this back then would have only served to make me even better at what I had the opportunity to do.

The communities and citizens directly affected in this case were lucky to have this group of people working for them. All the lost nights, the lost meals, the missed family events and the countless hours without sleep were all worth it.

*　　*　　*

My firefighters must be getting bored, I haven't given them much to do the past week. I have to find something to turn the red monster loose on.

September 17, 2004, nine days after the arsonist had let his friend, fire, out last. It was a cloudy, seventy-one degree morning in the Riverdale section of Prince George's County, and there was another fire. It was 0501 hours and the fire was set on the front porch of a single-family home, next to a main road with morning work traffic moving about. This fire presented a couple interesting things.

There was a person awake in the home and they were working on a computer just inside the front door where the arsonist set the fire. There was a large picture window just in front of the computer

SOLVING FOR X

Firefighters worked nightly to bring the arsonist's work under control.
Many of the scenes looked like this one.

in which the arsonist could have been easily seen. Second, there was a dog in a yard directly next to the target home and it would bark at anyone who came past the house. What this meant to me was our guy had to walk in from the main road or park just beyond the house away from where the dog was and do his work. He was bold enough to believe he could come in and set his fire and not be seen or caught. He was correct in his thoughts because nobody saw or heard him.

Our work in the neighborhood lasted well into the afternoon and then again that night and the next day, and the next week as it did with every fire. Like all the rest we came up with no hard evidence to identify our arsonist.

Three days later, Monday, September 20, at 0451 hours a fire was set at 2804 30th Street, Northeast in Washington, DC.

The location was just two blocks from the Evarts, homicide fire, where Lou Edna Jones died, and four blocks from the Channing Street auto fire and the Metro yard. *There must be some type of connection.* I did not know if it was a Metro employee, ex-employee, Metro cop or what. I did know that we had several fires near this Metro yard. We had one fire involving a Metro driver and a good bit of activity around this Metro yard. I began to look. I had to find what the connection was. I knew other members were looking at this angle but I wanted to be the one to find the clue that tied it all together.

I pulled all the fire reports we had and started searching for anything related: days of the week, times the fires were reported, any names that may have been in more than one report. I took a large moveable white board and began by placing the address of each incident on top. I then added each piece of information pulled from the reports. I had so many papers lying on the floor, one of my team members asked me if I was paper training a puppy.

I looked at street names to determine if the arsonist was using a pattern involving something from the names. I looked at the types of fires. I found out that Lou Edna Jones, the lady who died at the Evarts address, had a grandson who worked for Metro, and this made me even more interested about the Metro connection. I just needed to figure it out.

Thursday, September 23, 2004, at 0339 hours we had a request for the night crews to respond to an address in Wheaton, an affluent Montgomery County area not far from the DC border. Montgomery County is just like Fairfax, covering almost 500 square miles, a population over a million and very rich.

There is no way our guy would go out this far, I thought, but began driving in that direction. Just in case.

Shortly after fire units arrived, a callout was made: each supervisor was contacted and told of the new fire and the need for a response. A device was found in front of a garage door at 10817 Amherst Avenue. Everything found at the scene let us know it was our arsonist. The canvass and interviews lasted into the evening. Again we came away with nothing useful. *Why has the suspect moved to this location? Were we getting close to them? Did he need to expand his hunting area to have some new targets?*

Each time we had a pretty good net to catch this person, he made a change. The frustration was simply unreal. We had an earlier fire on the DC/Montgomery County border and we weren't sure if the arsonist knew he was in Montgomery County or not. This fire was well into Montgomery County. The investigation continued to move along and we were looking at as many things as we could think of, but we still weren't able to come up with a name of a good possible suspect.

The fires stopped after the September 23 fire in Montgomery County. We still had crews out at night covering as many areas as they could and responding to as many fires as they were able to, but none of them were the work of our arsonist. We found some set fires but none had our device.

We had many discussions about our arsonist. Setting fires is a compulsion and urge that's uncontrollable. The fire itself is a release for them. They have so much stress built up inside they have to use the thing that provides the release that they need and setting a fire is that release. We had one auto fire that we knew of where a device was used but no more.

In a supervisors meeting we discussed this.

Daley started, "Is this guy setting trash fires? Is he setting dumpsters on fire? Is he burning animals? He has got to be satisfying his urges somehow. We have to narrow the playing field. If our arsonist is satisfying his urge by setting cars on fire in both PG and DC we more than likely won't know it for a long time. If he goes to Virginia maybe we get lucky, they do investigate all vehicle fires but do not have near the numbers as their neighbors."

"I hate to be a dumbass in the group, but remind me why we won't know about car fires in DC and PG," I said.

"Bob, the *Reader's Digest* version is they have so many vehicle fires they don't respond to all of them like you Virginia boys do."

"Got it, sorry to have asked," I said.

121

We continued to look and hope; perhaps we would find a way to gain an edge. The Bladensburg Road area in Southeast, DC was an area where we had some fires and there was always a good bit of fire activity in the area as a whole. We asked DC to send investigators to all vehicle fires in this area just in case another car fire involved our device. We also asked DC to allow us to review the run logs from the two main stations that responded to this area, attempting to identify just how many fires we may have had there. Tom, Scott, and I visited both of those stations and spent a few hours looking them over. We copied down dates, address, times, types of vehicle if listed, and even the weather if it was in the log. We came up with a pretty large list that we would have to look at further.

We were advised that the director of ATF, Carl Truscott, would be visiting the Task Force command center on October 1. He was very interested in our case and not only wanted to see the setup of the Task Force, but wanted a briefing on the entire case. There had been one other such briefing provided to the director, and our boss—the Special Agent in Charge (SAC) of the Baltimore field office—did that. In the conversations I had been in with Theresa, she had proven she was all about her investigators and getting them what they needed to get the job done.

I recall one conversation we had shortly after I was assigned to the investigation. There were some issues with one of the agencies wanting to take back an investigator.

She told us, "Do not worry about that issue. I will talk to the chief of that agency. Do not give it another thought."

I also learned that she was not a person to be fooled with nor would she allow anyone to impede the efforts of her people. One time, we were on a fire scene and meeting some resistance from the local investigators. She approached them and basically said, "This can be done the easy way and you can assist us, or it can be done the hard way and we can obtain a federal search warrant and make it known to the public how difficult you have been." It got their attention real quick and there were never any additional issues.

I quickly learned that she was all about business and I could not have been happier that I was considered one of hers.

The SAC visited one of our morning briefings and advised the commanders that we would be making the presentation to Director Truscott. He was a tall, very trim man, who never appeared to have a hair out of place. He had done a couple tours as the head man in the presidential protection detail during his time in the Secret Service and had been appointed the Director of ATF by Attorney General Ashcroft. We were provided with the details of how the briefing needed to be prepared and what the director would expect. We had just a few days to prepare. I saw that it did not matter what level of government or business you are working in local, state, or federal—you never get much advance notice when the big boss wants something.

I felt a bit out of place as I would be face-to-face with a person appointed by the President of the United States and would be expected to provide him information about this case. I had been with many important people and never had a problem speaking, but I had never made any kind of presentation to a presidential appointee. As the day approached, everyone was making sure we had the place in good order, we didn't want this man to think we operated in a pigpen. Our work areas often become cluttered with way too many things we don't need. When there is an important visitor, staff never want them to think they are unorganized.

On the day of the scheduled briefing, everyone was in their jackets and ties, and we had all the information ready in neatly organized packets. There was fresh brewed coffee and the SAC brought in one of those nice decanters to serve it in. I made a mental note: *Make sure the director gets coffee poured from the nice stuff. The same everywhere you go.* There was an advance security team who arrived to make sure everything was in order. We believed our program was in order only to find that the advance team wished to change it just a bit. We were told who would be in the room when he arrived and just how we were proceeding. Everything must be done like a finely-oiled machine.

When the director arrived, he was friendly and engaged in some chat about general things before we started. As we prepared to sit at the conference table we found that our seating assignments were not part of our game plan and we didn't know where to sit.

Director Truscott tells me to sit next to him.

I say, "Yes sir." Yet in my head I'm saying, *Why in the hell did you have to pick me to sit next to you?*

It is not like the guy was going to bite me or anyone else in the room, but his position did command a great deal of respect and people are not placed in this type of situation everyday. I'm usually cracking jokes or busting someone's chops for stupid stuff and I couldn't do that sitting next to him and make a decent impression.

As things got underway, everyone took out their notes. I had arranged mine in a nice new notebook, making sure it was not too brightly colored, that it didn't have anything sparkly to draw attention to it. It was conservative, dark blue, and had a folder inside just in case there were handouts I needed to save. I wanted to be prepared for anything.

I looked next to me and found that Daley had his notes written in a green Harry Potter notebook with what looked like a lion's face in bright yellow on the front, and I laughed out loud, hoping I wasn't asked to say what was so funny. I had worried about the impression I would make on this man and wondered about how he would receive the information I had to report on, and one of my co-presenters was so relaxed that he had information prepared in one of his kid's notebooks.

In my head I was saying, *what the hell, Daley?*

It really didn't matter that the Director of ATF was visiting; our daily lives with our family is what really mattered. In the end I don't even think he noticed the Harry Potter notebook, but it sure has made for great storytelling when we talk about our past experiences and gave Daley a new nickname.

He later explained, "I didn't have much free time to prepare my notes. I was helping one of my kids with homework and I made my notes in that notebook."

During the briefing session, I was a bit surprised that the director, a man in control of one of the most important law enforcement agencies in the country, seemed to know such a great deal about our case. I know that as the boss he is supposed to know, but the questions he asked were not the typical administrative things you would expect, he was asking investigative questions. When he asked about the device and how we thought the arsonist was getting small purchases of gasoline and going unnoticed, I knew this was the kind of person I would want to work for.

We laid out several new initiatives we wanted to employ, including looking at vehicles more closely and using infrared detection. Using infrared cameras on aviation units in a particular area we would be able to tell which vehicles still had warm motors. We said we needed additional staffing if we were to be successful.

When the event was over, Theresa informed us how impressed Director Truscott was with what we had to say and the work we were doing, and said we could expect the staffing we requested. She went on to tell us this case had become of personal interest to him, since it began right after his appointment. The director wanted regular briefings from this point forward and we were told he would be sending questions to us from time to time.

This meeting pointed out that the case had gone beyond that of a local or regional case. This was a major investigation that had people watching on a national level. Now there was even more added pressure to close it with an arrest. Everyone involved in the investigation had been placed in a pretty difficult situation. If we failed to make an arrest, and the arson fires continued to happen, we all became failures in our profession. If we made an arrest, would we have done our jobs good enough and built a solid enough case to gain a conviction. All I could think was, *don't allow yourself to dwell about these things or you will become so overwhelmed you won't be able to function but the fact remains these issues were there and none of us were in a pleasant position.*

CHAPTER 12
Syd's Drive In Liquor Store

On November 2, 2004, DC fire responded to an auto fire at Syd's Liquor store on Bladensburg Road, just across the street from the Metro bus barn. The vehicle involved, a black SUV, was owned by a Metro bus driver. Fire investigators found nothing unusual and did not inform the Task Force.

A week later, the Task Force received a call on the tip line from a person claiming to work for Metro. He told us the November 2 vehicle fire involved a Metro bus driver, who was the owner, and he had the vehicle set on fire. The caller also said he knew of other car fires and all were owned by Metro employees. While collecting the information on the most recent fire, we got a second call on the tip line and this caller told us about the suspected arsonist in the vehicle fire riding on a Metro bus and acting very nervous. We asked how they knew this information, they were not willing to say. We asked the caller where the person boarded the bus and where they got off, and the caller had answers to both questions.

We went into action and conducted lengthy interviews with both callers. While the information that any caller provided us remained confidential, we tried to obtain a callback number for each. This situation was a great example of why a contact number is so important. We also began to look at the owner of the vehicle which had been involved with the most recent fire and placed him under surveillance. We sent a team to watch his home in DC, a team to watch his mothers home in PG County, and a team to his workplace.

Fulkerson, Daley, and I had a conversation about needing more information on fires in the area.

"This guy just doesn't fall out of the sky and sets a house on fire every few days. There has to be something else satisfying his urges," Daley said.

"If we want to know what types of fires are happening in the area, we need to just go back and look at the log books in the area fire houses," I said.

"Can you explain a little more? I'm not up to speed on fire station log books a hundred percent," Fulkerson said.

"Basically it is the fire department's version of a law enforcement roll call. Everything that happens during the course of a day of importance is recorded in the log so the next shift can review it. Every response they have will be in the log book," I answered.

Tom chimed in, "There is a station just a couple blocks from Syd's Liquor. Why don't we just stop in and see what we can find?"

"Daley, how do you know there is a fire station so close by?" I said.

Daley responded, "I only know because there is an Irish restaurant across the street."

I just shook my head and laughed.

When we got to the station, I talked with the captain and told him what we were trying to do and he was fine with us looking at his log book. We only went back about six months but saw the address for the liquor store a couple of times.

Fulkerson made a great suggestion. "Why don't we ride over to the liquor store and just look around."

Daley was in true form, "I knew there was a reason you were the boss. Let's go."

We walked around the parking lot and noticed a burnt area on the ground, which appeared to be burnt plastic.

"Look at this, Daley. I wonder how long it has been here," I said.

Fulkerson noticed newly installed parking blocks and floodlights.

"These floodlights should have scared folks off," I said. "My guess is they weren't here for the fire."

"Bob, you have the makings of a great investigator," Daley said.

"You can kiss it buddy," was my response.

We decided to enter the store and talk to the person in charge. We got lucky and found the owner present. He informed us there had been several vehicles burned in his lot over the last year or so and he had installed the flood lights and parking blocks recently to try to reduce the activity. A couple of vehicles had been parked up next to the building and were set on fire.

Fulkerson asked him, "Do you have any video surveillance in your lot?"

"No sir, I don't. It costs too much."

"Can you tell us anything more about the fires?" Daley asked.

"No, I really can't."

"Ok, thanks for your time. We are going to just look around a bit if you're okay with that," Scott said.

We left and continued to look around. In the back of the lot, Scott noticed a surveillance camera on one of the locations next door.

We went to the business but it was closed for the night. We marked down the name and address and knew someone from the night crew would be assigned to visit first thing in the morning.

Walking to the rear of the liquor store, we found a group of Metro drivers having an after-work gathering. Daley approached them, identified who we were, and started asking questions.

"Do any of you guys know anything about the car fire that happened last week?"

The group just laughed collectively. One guy spoke up, "Man, more than one car burned in this lot."

Another guy drinking a tall boy in a brown bag said, "This is the place to get your car burned."

We couldn't believe what we were hearing. Everyone seemed to know about the vehicles being burned and they indicated there may have been as many as twelve to fourteen. We wanted more information

but it became evident very quickly the group was hesitant to say much.
I tried to ease their concerns.

"Guys, we don't give a damn about what you're doing. If I wasn't
on duty, I would have one with ya. Everyone needs a cool beverage
after work. We are just trying to learn about the cars burning here."

The just-one-of-the-guys approach worked. When we left, we had
information on three or four of the fires and had eight names of people
who either knew more or had their cars burned. We even had types
and colors of cars that we could use to match to the run logs. It would
seem we had a pretty good plan and that it was coming together.

We finished and returned to the command center well past 2000
hours. A detective from DC who was working the night shift was
contacted and asked to be at the location on Bladensburg Road that
had the video camera when it opened. If he found the right footage,
he was to bring it to the command center for our morning briefing at
0800 hours.

When I arrived at the command center the following morning,
the night shift detective was already there but didn't have any tape. He
had seen the video footage and described what he saw.

"The footage did in fact show the person we had under surveillance
driving his SUV into the parking lot. This person got out of the
vehicle and a second person got out of the passenger side," he said.
"Together, they removed a bicycle out of the back and then the driver
walked away. The second person removed a gas can, walked to the
driver's side and then rode away on a bike. He appeared to go south
on Bladensburg Road."

"Seconds after leaving on the bike there were puffs of smoke seen
and then the vehicle erupted into flame."

Could this be our arsonist? My mind was going in a hundred
different directions. *We had one other fire scene where a guy was seen
on a bike. We are having a meeting with DC fire today and will discuss a
plan of action and get some answers.*

During the meeting with DC, Sergeant Gamble of their

investigations unit, informed us they really did not know about this case until we called to inquire. He went on to say the initial case investigator had completed his work and turned in the case report, which had been reviewed by a supervisor and assigned to the investigators to follow up on, but not much else was known or had been done. We all agreed the Task Force would need to pick up the owner of the vehicle that burned and interview him as soon as we could find him. We wanted very much for DC fire investigations to be a part of that process. We left the meeting feeling pretty good, knowing that not only would we be working to find this guy at our end, but DC fire investigators would as well. The sergeant knew we suspected this guy to be our arsonist. I left straight from the meeting and led a team of eight investigators in four cars to watch our suspect at work. I arrived at the Bladensburg Road location and immediately saw our subject was on the move.

I was alone in my vehicle and said out loud, "Wait! Everybody is not here yet. You can't move. We only have one car on site." I got on the radio and told everybody to hurry up and get there.

Too late. I saw the guy enter traffic and lost sight of him. I gathered my thoughts and told everyone he had left and to just set up surveillance at the home in PG county and the other home in DC. Cars split between the two locations and everyone was off.

I took the PG county location because that was the longest distance to travel and made me closer to my home if we ran late. When everyone arrived at their assigned locations, they found the suspect had not arrived yet. We hung around a couple of hours hoping he would show up. He was due back at work at 1300 hours and I told everyone to break, pick up their lunch, and be at the Bladensburg Road location no later than 1230 hours.

While riding to pick up my lunch, I got a call from Daley at the command center.

"Bob. I need you to drop whatever you're doing and get right over to Bladensburg Road bus barn!"

"What the hell is going on, Daley?" I asked.

"It seems that Gamble and the rest of the DC group may not have been as forthcoming as we thought when we met this morning. We were being told that their investigators are going to be interviewing the suspect today. Right now! We need to try and get ahead of them so we can stop the interview. Scott has already left and is trying to find them."

"How come Gamble or some other boss from DC doesn't simply tell them to stop?" I asked.

"I don't really have an answer for that, Bob. Sly is indicating that he is trying but the investigators aren't answering the radio, cell phone or returning a pager request," Daley said.

"That's bullshit," I shouted.

"Keep your head buddy, but get there as quickly as you can," Daley said.

"I will," was my response.

I decided to try the parking lot at Syd's Liquor store. It was directly across the street from the Metro yard and there is a clear view of the road in both directions. When I arrived, I found Gamble sitting in the parking lot.

"What are you doing here?" I asked

"I'm looking for my guys," Gamble said.

"It seems a bit odd that I was just with you not more than two hours ago and you were driving a totally different car. What's with that?" I asked.

I got nothing back in response. My thought was, *He would not be noticed if he changed cars?*

We both were too late, as the investigators were already inside the Metro building interviewing the suspect. It not only looked like they would not return a call to their supervisor but that their supervisor failed to inform them that the Task Force wanted to be involved with the interview.

I gathered my entire team in the lot and told them, "Let's move our cars so we can set up on all possible locations that lead away so we can keep an eye on this guy. The vehicle the suspect is driving was parked on Bladensburg Road. There have been some issues with DC and we have to be ready when this guy leaves the Metro yard. We must keep him in sight."

"What's going on Luckett?" Derek asked.

"DC is not being cooperative and we don't want to lose this suspect. Let's set up and we can talk about it more later."

Everyone got on post and reported they were ready. When the investigators finished their interview they continued to refuse to talk with Fulkerson and tell him what took place in the interview.

They left him standing on the sidewalk and drove off. Fulkerson chased them across DC in and out of traffic. They had been dispatched to another fire. When they arrived, Scott was right behind them. When he caught up to them he did not hesitate.

"Have you guys lost your mind? We are in the middle of a federal investigation."

"You might be, but you're not in ours," one guy said.

"I really don't want to get in a pissing contest with you but if you continue to withhold information from our case, I will be forced to place charges against you," Scott replied.

"You do what you have to. The case is ours and you can kiss our ass," the second guy said.

Gamble arrived and took the two DC investigators off to the side and spoke to them. He dismissed his folks and approached Fulkerson.

"Scott, I know you're pissed so let me try and turn this around."

"I'm listening, but you need to know this: if there is not full disclosure from you and your people immediately, charges will be filed."

"Relax, you will have your information," Gamble said. "The suspect had an uncle who works for DC fire. The suspect contacted the uncle and then the two of them met the investigators and the four of them spent the evening watching Monday Night Football and discussing the case. They made plans to interview him the next day. All the case file information will be in your hands by 1630 hours today."

"Gamble, if it's not, people will start being charged by 1700."

With that, Fulkerson turned and walked away without saying another word. When he got moving he called Daley and asked that he bring the other supervisors with him and meet around the corner from the Metro yard. When we gathered, it was easy to see he was in no mood to play around.

"We need to keep track of this guy. We have lost him once. We need a plan," Scott said.

Daley said, "Let's just put a tracking device on his car and be done with it."

"I'm in agreement with that but how do we get it there?" The vehicle is parked on the main road and there is a great deal of vehicle and foot traffic," Scott replied.

I made the following suggestion. "Just pull me over, and call me out and arrest me. While you are dealing with me, the tech guy can slip under the target's car and do his thing. The focus will be on me and my arrest and not what's going on under the suspect car."

It was agreed that was what we would do. The cover cars that were in place on both ends of Bladensburg Road were notified about the plan and told to keep a watchful eye out.

It was 1500 hours and rush hour would begin soon. We had to move immediately and get this thing done before there was too much movement on the street. I pulled onto Bladensburg Road and Scott and another agent pulled in behind me. As we approached the suspect vehicle, they turned on their lights and siren. I knew it was coming and it still scared the hell out of me! They got on the PA system and told me to get out with my hands in the air. While getting ready to get out I saw a DC police patrol car approaching. We had forgotten to tell them. I hesitated getting out, they slowed, but were told it was all right and they could move on. When the patrol car moved off, I got out of my car and walked backwards to the rear of my vehicle, hands in the air. I'm thinking, *This has to look good and everybody has to be watching us, right? I can't look around now—I'm being arrested.*

Fulkerson and the agent go through the entire deal, pat me down, read me my rights, and then handcuff me. They had to enjoy this as they put them on extra tight and double locked. They placed me in the back of Scott's car and the other agent got in my vehicle and drove off.

Just before they removed me from the rear of my car, we could see a lady walking up the sidewalk. She was looking at us but the tech guy was coming out from under the suspect car. When we arrived back at our agreed upon location there had been calls about the events over the radio and we looked at our laptop and found our device was working great.

We tracked this guy for just another day or two and got all the issues talked out with DC. They provided all the case file information to Scott on time and understood any further actions like they had just gone through would be met with swift and direct attention. The Task Force supervisors met and we decided that this suspect should be brought in before the US Attorney in DC, as was done with all of their cases. This would also keep DC involved and hopefully show them we didn't want to take over their case unnecessarily. Tom and a DC detective interviewed the guy, and he admitted he paid someone to set his car on fire.

The suspect he identified was an old friend with a criminal history with drugs. He was paid one hundred dollars to set the vehicle on fire. The Metro driver was behind in payments and wanted out. We looked for the suspect who had set the SUV on fire for a pretty long time with no success, so we turned him over to the US Marshal Fugitive squad to locate. He was looking at ninety-eight months backup time for drug charges.

We were able to determine that this case was isolated and those involved were not part of our arson case. We still had the other fires at Syd's to look at. DC fire provided the case files on the six cases we had identified, two of which were determined to be arson, three determined to be accidental, and one was undetermined. There was nothing more found to assist us in our case. The incidents that were arson did not mention any device in the case file. A good try and nice diversion, but still we came up empty.

As in any investigation involving this many people from this many agencies, things are not going to go smoothly all the time. To say we did not have problems during our investigation would be a lie. There were times people within the Task Force did not get along. There were times that fingers were pointed at each other over some trivial point. There were issues with local investigators versus federal investigators. There were times that people got their feelings hurt. Many people tried to make news out of this with no success. Things happened, were dealt with, and we moved on. For example, shortly after my arrival to the Task Force I was approached by one of the ATF supervisors.

"Bob, one of my agents has come to me and said that he felt you should be removed from the case. You were a local fire marshal and had no idea what you were doing as a supervisor."

I got pissed. "This agent and I had butted heads over his leads and what he was or was not doing," I said. "When I asked for updates, he told me that he did not have to answer me. His supervisors knew what he was doing and he said that was all that mattered."

I then told the ATF supervisor, "Bill, I don't mean any disrespect to you, but I'm not going to answer any more of your questions. I suggest you talk with the people assigned to my team and if you come away with the feeling that your agent was correct and I have no idea about what I'm doing, I will gladly leave the Task Force." The agent who made the complaint was transferred within a couple of days.

If you were to bring members of your family together in the same location for two years, do you think you would not have problems? Look, there are issues when you get together for the holidays or reunion so it is unrealistic to think that adults who have a particular way of thinking and doing things are always going to get along, when someone else is asking them to do things differently than the way they think it should be done.

As long as the majority of people involved can remain focused on the task at hand, the other things that happen are simply diversions that last a day or two or even a week or two, but they pass. I cannot find anything useful in spending time harping on the issues we faced. Each individual must look himself or herself in the mirror and ask if they did all that they could do to make the investigation a success. If they can walk away saying yes, then that is all that really matters.

I faced a range of challenges during my assignment and I tried to meet every one of them with the same mind set.

We all have to track and arrest the arsonist, doing whatever it takes, and not detract from the work the unit was doing. I was but a very small piece of this puzzle, but I never wanted to be the piece that prevented something positive from happening.

Our overnight surveillance sessions were spent running from fire scene to fire scene. An auto fire in DC and then another in Maryland, back to DC for a house fire then over to Virginia for a house fire. We were logging many miles a night just trying to keep pace and making sure we were looking at as many scenes as we could. Our nights began just before midnight when we would all meet at the command center in PG County. A shift consisted of eight people, including one supervisor. Four vehicles with two people in each. One vehicle was assigned to DC, one to Virginia, one to PG, and a supervisor who would ride in all areas, including Montgomery County.

One particular night we all left our meeting point about the same time and headed out on Route 295. There is a particular portion right near the border between DC and PG county, where the road splits. If you go in one direction it leads directly down to Bladensburg Road in DC, and if you go the other way, 295 will take you to the famed Woodrow Wilson Bridge that connects Maryland and Virginia. Two vehicles left heading toward Virginia, two of us went toward Bladensburg Road.

Just as we hit the split, I saw a small compact car rolling to a stop in a grassy area off to my left and another car picking up speed off to my right. I was riding with an agent from Kentucky and we quickly turned on my emergency lights and pulled over to see what had happened.

We exited the car and saw three guys emerging from a wooded area yelling about people being shot. We were not sure what was going on. *Should we take cover?* We ran to the woods to check and found a younger black male lying in the woods with a gunshot wound in his side. There was a second back male complaining of a gunshot in his rear and two others who were just mad about being shot at. I ran back to my car and got on the radio and requested assistance from PG County.

We were in a very unique location right on the PG/DC line and the roadway we were on—the Baltimore Washington Parkway—belonged to the United States Park Police. As I finished my request, I saw two additional men emerging from the woods, they had guns drawn and I yelled at my partner and took cover as I drew my weapon and tried to determine who the hell they were.

The two men turned out to be investigators from my team who were going to Virginia. They saw me stop and turn my lights on and came back to check on us. The other vehicle with two team members, who were going toward DC, had also witnessed the car rolling to a stop and the one speeding up. They radioed me that they had that car stopped and had pulled three out of the car under gun point and were checking them out.

I ran back to the woods and along with Barry, an investigator from Fairfax County Fire and Rescue in Virginia. We began immediate care of the two gunshot victims. In a pretty short amount of time we were surrounded with law enforcement officers from several agencies and were able to back out of the craziness. We all gathered at my vehicle and waited for the interviews to begin. Once the wounded were loaded into medic units and taken away and investigators were able to begin to interview folks, the scene quickly cleared. We were required to go back to the US Park substation to complete our interviews and fill out statement forms.

Once we were released from the scene, we were told it would be an hour before the detective handling the interviews would arrive.

"Ok guys, let's get a quick bite before we go to the interview," I said.

"There is a Waffle House just up the street from the Park Police substation," Brian said.

"Lead the way, Brian."

I radioed our last team and informed them of what happened and invited them to eat with us.

After two hours of interviews and paper writing, we were released. It was about 0530 hours and we had not been able to run any fires. I was glad we didn't get any radio requests to respond to anything. I told everyone to go home and get some rest.

The cause of this little encounter were two groups of people in Prince George's County who had a running feud and had been fighting for several months. There was another confrontation, and after that, there was a follow-up drive-by shooting. In fact, one of the guys who was shot in this incident had been shot about eight months prior in another similar incident. The people in the car we saw speeding away were not the shooters, but friends of the guys that were shot. They were just trying to get away from the area before they were shot.

As I began my drive home and had a little time to reflect, I wondered what the hell I had gotten myself into. I was a local town fire marshal. I had made a multitude of arrests and conducted tons of investigations, but nothing rising to this level. I had a staff of seventeen who went out on a daily basis and handled things: writing criminal summons, investigating house fires. They dealt with people upset over a repair to a sprinkler system or closing some commercial locations for non-compliance. They didn't as a matter of routine pull people out of cars at gunpoint or deal with multiple gunshot victims.

Then it really hit me. I was no longer that local town fire marshal;

I was a federal law enforcement officer and I had to be prepared to deal with any type of incident that happened. I might be looking for a person who is setting fires in three states, but my job covered much more than that.

When I got home I could not go to sleep, I was much too worked up and had way too much energy. I hooked the dog up to her leash and she got an extra-long walk. We walked along the path behind my home in the woods. It was peaceful, the day just beginning for the animals. I passed a few joggers who looked me over pretty good. I had not changed out of my work clothes and still had my gun and assorted gear on. When I got home, my wife greeted me with a warm hug. She always knew when I had one of those days. She never pried, but quietly let me know she was there if I needed to talk.

Being a criminal investigator is truly unique and not many outside of it can fully understand what we do or how we do it. There had been several changes in where and how our arsonist was setting fires. We had to deal with the addition of vehicle fires and trying to cover all the geographic areas having fires. The Task Force was working extra-long hours to solve for x, but had no real idea of when or how it would happen. We continued to follow up on our leads, cover the overnight shifts and continued to work to solve the case, having no idea how long it would take.

CHAPTER 13
The Red Herring

The months of October and November came and went without much action. There were a couple of fires in Prince George's County near the end of November, close to the University of Maryland in College Park. They received a great deal of media attention because both were well known to local residents as well as the university. The first fire took place at a motel about 0530 hours. The second occurred not more than an hour later and within sight of the first.

The second incident involved a local food and drink establishment. This location burned to the ground. We sent many members of the Task Force to both locations but investigators determined the fires were not part of our investigation, but both fires were set. Our investigators were requested to remain involved and were tied up for several days assisting.

We were working to put together a list of items we could take public for one more appeal for help, including the latest sketch of the suspect and more details about his profile. Agents from around the country were still rotating in to assist every forty-five days.

One of the agents from Philadelphia told us about a case in which they conducted a hypnotism of a witness and were able to gain additional valuable information.

This brought about a conversation at our morning briefing which lasted longer than it should have.

"There is no way this could work," Padgett said.

"Making people act like a chicken is not part of what we do," Chapman said.

Billy suggested, "We don't have anything to lose."

There were issues with our attorneys not wanting to damage the credibility of our witness.

Finally Scott said, "I appreciate all of the input. Everyone has made their point of view known in excellent fashion as you always do. We need to be able to tell the powers that be that we have done everything possible to close this case successfully. With that in mind, this is what we are going to do. I'm going to contact the doctor, a psychologist, and the agent who conducted these sessions and ask several questions. While I'm doing this, Daley will be talking with Ricky, Jerome, and Reggie to determine their interest."

As you could imagine, the brothers did not warm to the idea right away. Everyone had these preconceived ideas about being hypnotized, and our young men were no different. Daley assured them they would not be made to bark like dogs or made to do something foolish. It would simply be an interview session with two men in a very controlled and comfortable location. Supervisors met and decided we still had some work to do to convince the brothers. The investigators assigned to the boys would continue to talk to them and try to calm their fears. In the meantime, we would work to make this hypnotism happen. Scott would continue to communicate with the doctor and agent and find a date to conduct the interviews.

On December 5, 2004, there was a fire in Arlington County, Virginia. It occurred at a single family home located at 301 North Bryan Street. This was a small, quiet community right off Route 395 near the Pentagon. The incident took place in the early morning hours and the Task Force was not called at the time of the fire. The next day the captain in charge of fire investigations for Arlington County contacted me.

"Hey Bob, how have you been? We had a fire that appears to have been a candle wrapped with some type of cloth that had been soaked in what smelled like gasoline. The candle had then been placed on the top step of a rear deck on the home and set on fire."

"Tom, I'm at the Task Force so I'm going to put you on speaker so everyone here can listen. Was anybody hurt?"

"No injuries and the homeowners discovered the fire and called 911. While conducting our canvass of the area, investigators found a pair of Marine Corps dress pants lying in the road. The pants were about a block from the fire and smelled like gasoline. They also found a Marine Corps dress cap and a pair of white socks that looked like that may be something worn with a dress uniform. The socks were found in the yard next to the house where the fire took place and the hat not far from the pants."

Scott spoke up, "Captain, I really appreciate you getting in touch with Bob. If more people would reach out to us, it sure would make our job easier. I have to tell you that based on what you have said, I'm not of the opinion that this fire is related to our case. The fire was set on the steps of an outside rear deck. There is a candle wrapped in a cloth and not a plastic jug. You say items smell like they had been soaked in gasoline and in all our cases a liquid is present. There really is nothing connecting the dots for me."

"Ok, no worries, guys. I just wanted to run it by you," the Arlington Captain said.

"Since we had two other fires where there were some types of pants present, perhaps we should have your collected evidence transferred to the ATF lab and have them examined just the same."

"Can you also provide us with a copy of the case jacket and associated pictures. This way our procedures stay intact," I said.

"Whatever you need, Bob."

"Thanks for calling. Someone will be in touch with you later today and get that evidence picked up," I said.

Once I was off the phone, Scott spoke again.

"That was interesting, but I'm not feeling it. Call the Falls Church office and request that they get in touch with Arlington. Arlington can then make the transfer to them which would both keep the chain of custody correct and if the fire is not connected as I believe, then that field office and the agent that was assigned can remain involved with Arlington while they gather additional information."

"No worries boss, I will call right now," I said.

I called the Resident Agent in Charge (RAC) in Falls Church and covered what we had and why we thought we should follow our established procedures. She advised me that she would assign it to someone and the evidence would be picked up immediately. A few hours later the agent assigned to pick up the evidence called and questioned me as to why this really needed to be done. I explained that we were just being safe and while he may think it was a waste of time, that the items still needed to be picked up and transferred.

On December 6, a vehicle was set on fire on 11th Street Northeast DC and the location was about two miles from other recent fire locations. We had units on the street working the overnight detail of chasing fires. Brian, the very outspoken PG detective, was working as the acting shift leader that night and got on the scene just after the fire department. He was on scene so quickly, DC investigators were upset that the Task Force was trying to take their incidents away from them. Brian was able to get a look at the vehicle and quickly determined that a device was there. He had the overnight group respond to the area. The entire Task Force was called out. The fire took place at 0411 hours, so by the time everyone was on the scene it was almost daylight.

Everything that had taken place with the DC fire investigators had been worked out and the Task Force was working under the impression that everything was okay. The same two investigators who had caused the earlier problems with the SUV that was set on fire at Syd's Liquor were handling the call for DC. When they arrived, they immediately roped off the area with crime scene tape.

Brian was in a rare form. "It's four in the morning. Who the hell are you trying to keep out?"

"You step inside that tape and you will find out who!"

"Scott, this is Padgett. The two idiots from DC are here and have told us that anybody who comes inside the tape will be dealt with harshly. Can I deal with them my way?"

"Brian, I will be there in ten minutes. Just have our people back off and I will deal with those guys when I get there."

"Scott, this is bullshit, these guys are just being assholes."

"Brian, we don't need a fight in the middle of somebody's yard. Please just wait a few minutes."

"OK, but if they come near me, all bets are off. I saw the device and know this is our case."

When Scott arrived he spoke with the investigators in a very hushed tone.

"Gentlemen, we have been on a similar road once before and I allowed your boss to work things out. Today, that will not happen. You become one hundred percent cooperative right now or I will direct my Task Force to arrest you both. Don't interpret this as a threat. Understand it is a fact. Now, may we move forward?"

"All you feds want to do is take all our calls. Have at it," one of the DC guys said.

In the end, the evidence was transferred over and we completed our usual scene processing and neighborhood canvass. We learned the victim of this fire was a Metro employee and used to work at the bus barn on Bladensburg Road. While at the scene, we got word of a very large fire involving multiple single family homes in southern Maryland. The fires were about twenty to thirty miles from our location and many within the Task Force were put on standby to respond and assist. These fires would later turn out to be one of the worst in the history of the state of Maryland and remained in the news for several days. The arson occurred in Charles County, Maryland. A subdivision called Hunters Brooke with a few homes built and several more under construction were targeted. A pre-dawn incident where a total of thirty structures along four streets were either set or attempted to be set on fire. In the end, five men were arrested and later convicted of a racially-motivated act.

Once the recovered evidence from the 11th Street auto fire was moved to the lab, investigators found some writing on a bit of a black plastic bag found in the debris.

The writing said: *Made in China for the Cornelius Sho-*

Based on this, we researched on the internet late into the night trying to find out what this writing was all about. We were able to locate a Cornelius Shoppe in England. Through a collateral request to the United States Secret Service, arrangements were made to conduct an interview with the store owner in England. The Secret Service said they would handle the interview pretty quickly. We waited for the results of their efforts.

The day after the auto was burned, there was another fire. This one was located in the Bladensburg section of Prince George's County.

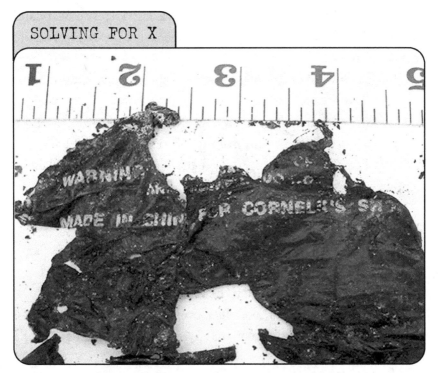

SOLVING FOR X

Partial remains of the black bag with white text
(Image courtesy of the author's files)

The call came in at 0508 hours and involved a garden-style walk-up apartment building. We immediately assumed that since the fire that occurred in southern Maryland was getting so much attention in the news, our arsonist must have decided he would not be outdone. The device had been placed in the stairwell between the first and second floor, blocking all passage from the upper floors. There was a light rain falling and it was very cold, but firefighters made quick work of the fire.

Three days later in Northeast DC, Task Force investigators found a device on the front porch of a single family home. The device was next to the front door and under a very large picture window.

We had investigators nearby; in fact, a group was just around the corner having coffee at a 7-11 and heard the call go out over the radio at 0454 hours.

When I arrived, the night group was buzzing. Derek, a Maryland State Fire Marshal, didn't even give me time to get my gear on before he was in my ear.

"Luckett, two of us had just come off that street before we went to the 7-11. The arsonist had to see us."

"Ok, slow down a bit. Who was with you?"

"Barry was with me. I know this guy had to see us."

"I heard you the first time. Go get Barry please, and we will cover all of it."

Standing at the command post, I told Fulkerson, Hoglander, and Daley what I had just been told by Chapman.

"Guys, our people had to see this guy or he sure had to see them. They were on this street just before the call was dispatched."

"Bob, where were they when the call went out?" Daley asked.

"They were at the 7-11 one block over, Tom."

"It sure would seem likely that somebody saw somebody," he answered.

Derek and Barry showed up a few minutes later and recounted all they did.

"We had been riding for several hours and the night was boring. We knew it was getting near the end of shift so we decided to get a cup at the 7-11."

"Barry, did you guys see any vehicles moving on the street?" I asked.

"Nope, and we only passed one old guy walking his dog. That's it."

"Did either of you notice anybody sitting in a car or a car with brake lights on?"

"I swear, Bob, neither of us saw a damn thing and that's what is pissing me off so much. This guy was right under our nose and we didn't see anything," Derek was fuming.

"Ok fellas, be sure you put everything that happened in a report before you head home so we have it all. There is nothing more you can do now. Go get some rest."

During the evidence collection process we were able to identify a black plastic bag and quickly determined that it was similar to the one recovered at the December 4 fire. This time investigators were able to piece together the entire wording found on the bag: *Made in China for Cornelius Shopping Bags Inc. U.S.A.*

Using laptop computers on the scene, we were able to determine that Cornelius Shopping Bags, Inc. was located in Richmond, Virginia; we dispatched two investigators to drive the 100-plus miles right away.

They found the bags were distributed to just two stores in the Maryland, DC, Virginia region. We identified both as being Circle Seven stores owned by the same individual. One store was located in Northeast DC and the other located in Southeast DC.

We devised a plan and sent people to speak to the store owner to gain his cooperation. We were not one hundred percent sure at this point if he or one of his employees were not involved, so we invented a story about armed robberies in the area. We knew at least one was robbed with some deal of regularity and we quickly gained his cooperation. Video surveillance in both stores was established. We believed the store in Northeast DC was the primary store because it

SOLVING FOR X

The second black bag recovered
(Image courtesy of the author's files)

was so near the Anacostia address that you could walk there. We also established a surveillance location from a nearby apartment complex. We would begin to send staff to this location daily.

At the morning briefing the next day, Fulkerson asked everyone to hang tight for a few minutes.

"Starting tonight and going forward until further notice, every night there will be a minimum of four investigators conducting surveillance on the Circle Seven stores. Two will be inside an apartment watching video surveillance and two will remain mobile. When the team inside identifies someone purchasing a one-gallon jug, they will attempt to gain a tag number from the car they are seen getting into. It is our theory that the arsonist will return to one of these stores in the future to purchase additional components for his device and when he returns, we will be waiting and watching."

"Is this overtime?" asked Brian, the PG detective.

"Brian, as long as you meet your regular 8-hour day, yes, it will be overtime."

"Where do I sign up?"

"Don't worry, my friend, there will be plenty for everyone."

"Scott, you are so good to us. Thank you."

The room erupted into laughter.

The apartment we obtained for surveillance was not in a great section of DC. This was a very high crime area with lower income level homes. We spent the entire Christmas holiday using this apartment in hopes our arsonist would return. My wife was not really pleased with me being out several nights a week, all night. Especially during the holidays. I tried never to work more than two nights in a row to keep the peace. The detail itself was not that bad. There was heat, an indoor bathroom, and we even managed to bring in a recliner so one person could nap. The detail was from 2200 hours to 0700 hours.

I usually worked this detail with a PG County police sergeant, Hank Anderson, who was as big as a house standing almost 6-feet-7-inches and tipping the scales at about 325. He had more years on the job than anyone on the Task Force, which meant I usually just kept my mouth shut and learned. Hank was a wealth of knowledge. He was hilarious as hell in a dry sort of way. He never moved fast but all of his movements had purpose. We split our duties evenly. Our first night together, Sgt. Anderson laid everything out for me.

"Bob, I feel comfort is our most important thing. If we are comfortable, we will work smarter and if we are comfortable we won't be worried about the normal surveillance issues, like going to the bathroom."

"I copy that, Hank."

"We will take turns each night on who is bringing the movies so we each can pick the ones we like. Comfort, Bob, comfort. On the night I bring the movies, you bring the snacks and on the nights you bring the movies, I'll bring the snacks."

"I'm loving this plan so far."

"Over my more than 25 years, I have learned that once you have the important things covered, everything else just seems to fall into place. Understand what you're eating and what your entertainment is has always been vital to being able to stay awake."

On the second night I worked with him, I realized my stupidity. Shortly after we got inside our second floor apartment, Hank asked me, "Do you own a ballistic vest?"

I answered, "Of course!"

"Where is it and how come you're not wearing it?"

"Sarge, I parked just outside the door and only had to walk the two flights to get inside here and I knew we were not going anywhere until 0700 tomorrow," I replied.

"Well, is that so?!"

"Yes sir, it is," I said, certain of myself.

"You listen, and listen well," Hank said. "You are in one of the worst sections along the DC/PG border. Every person living in the complex knows that you are the police and you are in this building. There are any number of people in the area who could and would gain a great deal of street cred if they shoot one of us. It only takes a fraction of a second for someone to drive by and fire a few rounds and kill you, and nobody is the wiser, even though you have just a few feet to walk to the entry door. Don't you ever take your or my safety for granted again, you understand me?!"

"Hank, I'm sorry. I never thought about that. All I can say is thank you."

"Bob, we are partners and what each of us does affects the other. My experience lies in the law enforcement arena and yours in the fire investigation game. If we continue to work at it, we will be a force to be dealt with."

"Neither one of us is a very small guy; I think we can handle most of what comes our way," I said.

"As long as you wear your vest, I think you may be right."

"Yes sir, you will never have to remind me again. Now can I ask what movies we are watching tonight?"

"You have quickly learned grasshopper," he said smiling.

We both said at the same time: "Comfort, it's all about comfort."

One night just after Christmas we were working together and heard a large amount of gun fire coming from the courtyard in front of our building. We ran to the front window and opened the blinds enough to see what was going on. Just a few teenage kids firing their Christmas presents into the air. Those few kids had way more fire power then we did. I looked at Hank and thanked him again. He just laughed.

On two occasions while watching the video monitors in the store from our apartment, we saw the location get robbed at gunpoint. Luckily, we had cars on the outside and were able to get marked units there quickly and effect arrests.

We spent many days trying to devise our plan for catching the arsonist, developing what became known as the "Black Bag Operation." We knew our surveillance operations were doing pretty well, but we needed a way to identify where our bad guy was getting his materials for the device. We decided we needed to isolate each store in case our guy preferred one over the other and used something from either one. We needed a way to determine which store's material was at the scene of the fire.

There had to be something that would remain after the fire was out that could tell us which store was used. We decided we needed a numbering system and we needed some type of metal to put the numbers on. We went to the lab and conducted some rather crude testing. We took some different types of steel and held a torch to them, trying to determine which would last in a fire. We talked to welders and learned that stainless steel would survive.

Then we figured out that if we had steel with a number on it we could use a metal detector and scan the debris and we would hand sift that pile to find our numbered metal.

We found a local shop that made numbered tags about the size of a dime and we placed an initial order for 10,000. We then made an initial order of 10,000 black plastic bags from the same company that made the ones we had been finding at the fire scenes. We would place these small stainless steel tags in the bottom of each bag. The numbers were split to ID each store. High numbers to one store and low numbers to the other.

We made arrangements with the stores that only one-gallon jugs would be placed in these bags. We now had to create a device for the bags to sit on which would be different from the rest of the bags. We initially obtained some bag holders from a local restaurant supply location, but soon found that they were not much different from what the store had and bags were getting mixed up. One agent on the Task Force had an engineering degree, so he built four dispensers: two for use and two for replacements.

The dispensers were made with plastic tops from coffee cans to hold the bags in place. A hole was cut in the center of the tops and a large rod was run through. The bags were placed on the rod and then held in place with some type of hinge. Really different but very effective. When there was a purchase with one of our bags, the theory was it would be used as part of a device. The stainless steel chip would remain after the fire. We would use metal detectors to locate the chip and identify the store from which it came. To better identify the numbers of one-gallon jugs being sold and which store they were coming from, we made daily trips to the stores at 0600 hours and picked up a bag. This way we were able to know daily how much was sold and how bags were used.

Each morning at our 0800 briefing, we would spend at least one hour setting up the bags. It was always a ball-busting session because everyone really hated the simple mindless process.

Folger started on me, "Luckett, you think you can turn a bag inside out and remember how to get it back to the right way?"

"I'll have you know that I'm an expert at this bag turning stuff."

"Really! Is it something they teach you at the retirement home?"

SOLVING FOR X

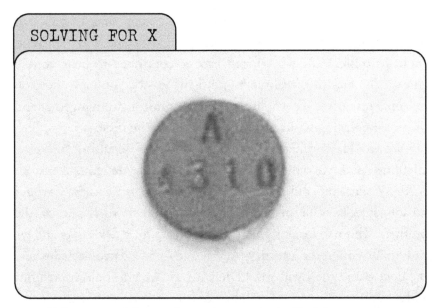

Enlargement of the stainless steel tag use in the black bag operation.
(Image courtesy of the author's files)

"Actually, I learned it during a class for the talented and gifted."

"I would have loved to see that class."

"Well next time, I will make arrangements for you to attend."

The process consisted of turning the bags inside out and taping one of the metal chips to the bottom. Done by hand the bag was then smoothed back out and placed on the dispenser. Each and every person assigned to the Task Force, including supervisors, performed this task. Once the bags were completed, the numbers of the metal chips were recorded on a calendar, so we would know what high numbers and low numbers were used on any given day.

We finished 2004 with a small gathering and some gag gifts exchanged. Tom got a Harry Potter wand, Brian was given a muzzle, and Scott was given a gavel so he could keep better order in our meetings. While it was not talked about much, we hoped we were moving in the right direction. No one expected this case to last this long. The holidays brought a good bit of talk and rumors about people being transferred or agencies leaving all together. With the Task Force not having much fire activity, it would be a good time to pull staff back and not receive much backlash. January came and went and we had no fires. The talk of staff leaving continued to increase. We entered the month of February and Scott was beginning to develop one final initiative. We would pull all of our information together and present everything we had to the public one more time.

We would see where that took us, and if we could not develop anything solid, we would consider downgrading the case to just an ATF investigation cold case and the Task Force, as we knew it would no longer exist. One of our final steps would be to hypnotize the brothers. This had been in the planning stages for a few weeks and we had finally gotten the attorneys to agree and had a date selected where the doctor and the agent would be with us. We got it all worked out and set up a meeting in a local hotel for February 10, 2005. The doctor and the agent would be in one room conducting the session, and the remainder of the group would be in an adjoining room watching it on closed circuit television.

Because of the large number of people, we needed a suite. There must have been at least ten of us wanting to watch something we had only heard about but had never seen. I was so excited I couldn't wait for it to begin.

"Daley, this is gonna be really cool, right?"

"Bob, I know you think I'm some kind of wizard, but I have no idea what's going to happen."

"Come on, I bet anything you have talked to several people and know exactly what is going to happen."

"You are partly correct. I have talked to some folks about the process just to see if they thought it would be worth our time but I really don't know what's going to happen."

"OK, I'll buy that. Can you get them started? I can't stand the wait."

"Patience, big guy, you will get your money's worth soon enough."

"This is going to be better than the circus. I bought popcorn, drinks, and candy. Tom, comfort is a really important thing."

"Bob, I'm glad Sergeant Anderson has educated you on one of the finer points of law enforcement."

The doctor was a quiet and reserved man who presented himself as confident in what he did. The agent was so full of energy that I thought he could never sit still long enough to talk to anybody. He seemed too confident, so I was intrigued even more at how this team would work. We had the three brothers separated and riding around in cars with our staff so they would not get too anxious. They were taken out to eat and then to play video games while passing the time. We were only going to try two of three so there would always be one not damaged in the eyes of our attorneys. The attorneys had only agreed to this because we told them that one witness would not be subjected to anything with the doctor. That way, nobody could say the testimony had been altered.

The first witness, Jerome, a 17-year-old with his hair in braids, wearing jeans below his waist, listening to music in his headphones, was brought in. After a few minutes of being very nervous, he relaxed. As I watched, I saw him drop his head and his body appeared to go limp. It's hard to explain. He didn't go to sleep; I was just seeing a very relaxed person sitting in a chair. The doctor asked him questions to take him to the day of the incident and Jerome was talking about things he was seeing in real time. I was on the edge of my seat. The very things that happened that night when he and his brothers drove up in front of their house and saw the arsonist were happening all over again, just like it was happening right then. I was a bit confused to begin with because I had no idea this was how it worked.

"Daley, what is going on? Is this kid dreaming?"

"Shut up, Luckett, I'm trying to listen."

The doctor was asking the majority of questions and the agent was filling in the gaps with additional comments and questions. We were passing additional questions under the door. When they got to the point of asking about the looks of the suspect, our room became totally silent. I could hear my heartbeat in my ears. I saw people inch closer to the TV monitor with anticipation. The tension in the room was building and it was easy to see everyone was hoping for something big to come out of Jerome's mouth. He didn't disappoint us; he was able to present a pretty good picture of what the arsonist looked like. We also got one piece of information that we did not have before. Jerome told us the suspect was wearing a shirt that had some type of logo on it and it was on the left chest. After about forty-five minutes, the session ended and we all rushed into the room to see the picture that was drawn and the drawing of the logo. When everyone got the first look, there was total silence for a minute.

Padgett exclaimed, "This is fucking awesome."

The tension broke. Everyone was laughing and slapping high fives. I never believed that this was possible, and had I not seen it with my own eyes, would still not believe it worked. The second brother was brought in and the same process started. After several tries, the doctor and agent decided this fellow couldn't relax enough to go under, and the session ended. For all of the work and energy we put into having this done, we felt pretty good at what it yielded. When we went to the public, we would now have three drawings of our suspect. They all looked alike and yet they all looked different. *Will it help us or hurt us?* I thought about this often. Our next area to work on would be the reward money.

We managed to get the amount up to $50,000.00. When we went public, we wanted it to be one hundred thousand. There were several requests put into the ATF administration and we hoped to get it approved. The final piece of this tell-all public campaign focused on the car seen leaving the Anacostia neighborhood. Several agents obtained a listing of cars from the DC and Maryland DMVs. They were told to visit each address provided by the DMVs and if the vehicle was visible from the road, take a picture of it. These photos would be placed in books and we would bring the witnesses back in to look at the photos.

If they could ID the car, we would begin to work up that owner.

When there was another fire or a more pressing matter, this process took a back seat. We needed more staff and didn't have it. It was going to take several more months to complete.

There were no more fires throughout the month and the rumors we had heard before Christmas became a reality. Agencies began pulling their staff back from the Task Force. We were still working our night surveillance details, working what leads came in, and trying to finish what others left, but the staffing numbers were getting smaller and the work wasn't going away. There was talk that the *Washington Post* was going to run an article about the Task Force. This article was supposed to outline problems that had been encountered along the way with DC fire investigators and the Task Force.

Nothing could have been worse. Investigators were being pulled away and now some newspaper article was going to sling mud at us. The work the Task Force had done should not be diminished; it should be applauded. Each time some bump in the road came about, it was dealt with and we moved on. We didn't want something written that may be cause for more agencies to pull their staff back. I was feeling the pressure. Too much work had been done to have a poor story written and try to ruin it. We didn't need some local reporter trying to make a name for themselves putting a damper on the hard work of the men and women who had been dealing with this thing for two years.

The morning of February 28 was a windy, thirty-four degrees and the headlines in the *Washington Post's* Metro section were about problems within the arson Task Force.

It didn't go into any real specifics about issues between agencies, but did reveal many facts of the case not known to the public. The story never cited a source of the information and it really didn't matter.

What did matter was we now had to see what damage it would cause and keep preparing for our final push. The month of March flew by and there had not been any fires in the past ninety days. Things were starting to look bleak for the Task Force. Something positive needed to happen and happen quickly.

CHAPTER 14
Tightening the Net

Early April 2005: the Task Force was notified by the Montgomery County police department crime lab that DNA was recovered from the Marine Corps pants that had been collected from the fire in Arlington, Virginia. The fire happened in December and had not been part of our response. They contacted us and reported they had a fire on a rear deck with a candle. Marine Corps clothing had been found in the yard and a couple streets over from the fire.

DNA, deoxyribonucleic acid, is the hereditary material in humans and almost all other organisms. A person's DNA contains information about their heritage, and can sometimes reveal whether they are at risk for certain diseases. In law enforcement, DNA testing is often used to help solve crimes. There may only be a few drops of blood or a single hair left at the crime scene, but this is enough to get a DNA profile. If two DNA profiles match, there is a one-in-a-billion chance they are from different people, unless they are identical twins.

This DNA matched the DNA found on the other items related to our serial arson suspect. We were told this was touch DNA. The suspect had touched something from the Arlington County fire and left DNA. Touch DNA is left every time any of us touch something. Particles of skin, sweat, and other items from our chemical makeup are left behind. In my almost thirty years in the fire service, I had never heard of any cases where investigators in the US recovered and successfully used touch DNA in helping to solve an arson case. I thought that DNA would be consumed by the fire. This case proved otherwise. The Arlington fire was determined to be the work of our arsonist and after a closer look, the candle they described was determined to be plastic consistent with the same type used in one-gallon jugs. With this information, the Task Force determined that our suspect was a current or former Marine, or had strong ties to the Corps. Recovered evidence at the Arlington fire included a Marine uniform dress cap and Marine dress uniform pants and socks.

We scheduled a meeting with members of the Naval Criminal Investigative Services. We were determined to come away from this meeting with the name of the person matching our DNA. We wanted access to the Armed Forces DNA database in an effort to match our suspect profile with a member of the military. We knew we would come away with what we needed.

During the meeting, we found the military only stores the raw DNA taken from each member and only uses it for identification purposes when the person comes up missing. The DNA profiles are not placed into a database for query purposes. The military told us that if we had a name, they could run that against all the names they had to see if there was a match, but we didn't have a name.

Even though this was a setback, NCIS investigators made us aware of two arson suspects who they believed had been setting cars on fire almost three years prior. That information had been turned over to DC fire investigators but NCIS had not heard any more on it. Interestingly enough, one of those suspects lived very near one of our Target Circle Seven Express stores on Martin Luther King Avenue. The military informed us they had video of a car and a suspect, and provided us with the names of the two possible suspects.

We immediately set up surveillance on the suspect who was identified as Thomas Anthony Sweatt, a Black male with a date of birth of November 1, 1954. We watched his home, located in Northeast DC, and his place of work, a Kentucky Fried Chicken restaurant, located at the intersection of New York Avenue and Bladensburg Road, Northeast DC.

This was just blocks away from the June 2003 fire on Evarts Street, the Channing Street fire in September 2004, the Yoast Street fire in December 2004, the Metro bus barn, and other locations on our list.

A photograph of Thomas Sweatt was shown to all three witnesses from the Anacostia Avenue fire but none provided a positive response.

We found nothing in his background that would indicate this could be our guy; he had no major criminal record and the arrests he did have were for nothing related to fire. He had worked for KFC for twenty years, holding the position of manager. He had a quiet home life and he worked in a church. We just couldn't find anything to relate him to our case, but we stayed the course; he would be ruled in or out just like any other person who had come to our attention.

On April 19, 2005, Task Force investigators interviewed Thomas Sweatt at his place of employment. We decided they would try to get his DNA by pulling a ruse; they told Sweatt his name had come up as part of the serial arson case investigation and they would like him to look at a coat that was found at one of the fires and determine if it is his.

The investigators put on gloves and Sweatt put on gloves. When they had finished looking at the coat, the investigators just tossed their gloves on the ground and Sweatt followed the same practice. They continued to talk with Sweatt and at one point asked him if he was the serial arsonist.

"Why would I want to burn those beautiful homes when I am trying to be a homeowner myself?" he said.

He did not say "No!"

Investigators became so convinced that Sweatt was not involved that they asked him if he would be willing to give them a sample of his DNA. He agreed and they did swabs of his cheeks and took the sample to the Montgomery County police crime lab. Sweatt later told us he agreed to do this because he really did not understand DNA and thought it was something only related to blood and semen. It was decided that we would maintain static surveillance on Sweatt through the week and asked the lab to expedite the DNA check so we could move on.

On Monday, April 25, 2005, at 0900 hours, Scott was sitting in his office and received a phone call from the Montgomery County police crime lab.

The lab director simply said, "Sweatt's DNA is an **EXACT** match with DNA recovered at all of your locations."

These were the locations:

- 4115 Anacostia Ave., Northeast, DC

- 7700 Blair Road, Montgomery County, Maryland

- 2804 30th Street, Northeast, DC

- 301 North Bryan Street, Arlington County, Virginia

Scott couldn't believe what he'd heard and asked the director to repeat it again.

The lab director said, "I would be happy to."

Once he was off the phone, Scott gathered the Task Force commanders present and told them the news. He then contacted all the investigators assigned full-time and part-time and informed them they needed to attend a meeting at the command post at 1300 hours. Every investigator had their own thoughts.

I was driving to a meeting and was in line at a fast food drive- thru when Fulkerson called. The call went something like this:

"Bob, there's a meeting today at the Task Force command center at 1300."

"Okay. What's going on?"

"Can't talk about it. Just be there, okay?"

"Yes sir."

My thoughts went back and forth between wondering if the Task Force was going to be shut down or if we had come up with a positive identification of a good suspect. There had been so many ups and downs in the past eighteen-months and I tried to quiet my mind until I received the information at the meeting, but it was hard. I was so worked up I could not eat. I tossed my entire lunch in the trash. I called my scheduled meeting and made an excuse to cancel it. I was sick to my stomach and could not figure out what was so important that I could not be told what the hell was about to go on.

When I arrived at our building, there was a lot of buzz and everyone was telling one another what they were thinking. I tried to pump my fellow commanders for information, but if they knew, they held it tight to the vest.

When the meeting began, Theresa, the SAC from Baltimore, was in attendance and I knew the news was going to be important. Fulkerson wasted very little time.

"The lab called the Task Force and informed us the DNA from Thomas Sweatt was an exact match. We have our guy!"

A gag order was issued to every member of the Task Force to prevent leaks. Knowing we did not have much time before the word got out, the SAC took on the responsibility of informing each agency still involved in the investigation of the pending arrest.

There was a lot of work to get done and we needed to do it in very short order.

The command post would be staffed around the clock. Two teams were established to conduct 24-hour surveillance on Sweatt until his arrest and meetings were held with the U.S. Attorneys in Maryland, Virginia, and DC to discuss charging documents. There had been regular meetings since the investigation began and the attorneys with all of these agencies had been attending. During those meetings, everyone was friendly and in agreement about what we were doing in the investigation. Now, there did not seem to be any agreement on anything. Over the last two years, the meetings often discussed the process of capturing and interviewing the suspect. They centered around where the suspect would go to be interviewed—and by whom—and where he would be charged. There always seemed to be plenty of smiles and agreement on what was discussed. Now with an arrest getting near, there needed to be closed-door meetings with lawyers only to discuss the very same things. In all, it took almost two days to iron out everything.

The final agreement was that members of the Task Force and members of the DC police department would arrest Sweatt when he arrived at his place of employment in Washington, DC. The interview team consisted of Scott and Frank Molino, a DC Homicide Detective who had been a part of the Task Force since it began. These two would take Sweatt to an agreed-upon location for the ensuing interview.

On April 27, 2005, I was leading the surveillance team. It was sixty-three degrees with light wind, and I was sitting in my car down the street from Sweatt's apartment having a cup of coffee and munching a luscious honey bun full of white icing dripping from the edges. The entire team of eight had been in place for about an hour and we felt that we had all the avenues to exit the place well covered.

At 0830 hours, Thomas Anthony Sweatt walked out the rear door of the building, down the wooden steps, climbed into his little aqua green car, and left his home. I was taking a bite of my honey bun when my radio chirped and the word that our target was on the move was broadcast. Sweatt took us on a driving trip that I still talk about today. When Sweatt left his home that morning, he began by driving very erratically. We had been following him for two days and he drove a bit erratically every day. We were convinced he knew we were following him. As he left, he drove down his alley and turned left out to the main street. Instead of driving one block and turning onto Martin Luther King Boulevard, he made a quick right into another alley. He drove down this alley about two blocks and made another left turn. When the car tailing reached the corner, they radioed that someone else would need to pick him up. He was driving the wrong way on a one-way street. Washington, DC rush hour traffic is legendary and not very forgiving, but Sweatt drove like he could have cared less about the traffic around him. He not only took us the wrong way on a one-way street, he took us into traffic, drove a few blocks, and then made a U-turn heading back in the direction he had just come from. All the time we were following Sweatt, I was reporting back to the command post.

"Command, this is Luckett. He just turned on a one-way street going the wrong way."

"Command copies. Do you still have an eye?"

"That's affirmative Command. We are heading toward Malcolm X Avenue at about ten miles an hour."

"Command copies."

"Command, we just turned onto Alabama Avenue and passed St. Elizabeth's Mental Hospital."

"Command, I'm no genius but this is not the way to Sweatt's store."

"Bob, this is Tom, we are aware of that. Maintain your surveillance wherever he goes."

"I copy that."

We could not understand why he was not going to his store or where he was going. He ended up at a KFC on Marlboro Pike in Maryland near where the Washington Football Team stadium is for a store manager's meeting.

While we were setting up on the location, the Maryland State Fire Marshal was calling the SAC and telling her congratulations on the arrest.

"Why are you calling to congratulate me for something we have not done yet?" asked Theresa.

"I just heard it reported on the local news radio station and wanted to be the first to call you."

"Thanks, gotta run."

She walked into the command post as I was telling Daley that we were not in DC but in Maryland. Based on the fact that the suspect was acting strangely, he was not at the planned location, and we had no idea where he might go and now the media was reporting the information, we faced some safety concerns. The team was advised not to let the suspect get back on Marlboro Pike.

Daley asked, "Are you in a position to effect an arrest?"

"We can be within a few minutes," I replied, and then asked, "Does Fulkerson know about this?"

As I was radioing units to get into position, a transmission was made that the subject had entered his car and was pulling off of the lot. I was in a church parking lot directly across the street from the KFC and flew to the street with lights and siren to block the exit.

When I opened the door to my vehicle and identified myself, Sweatt seemed a bit confused and in shock. I told Sweatt to turn the car off and place both hands on the steering wheel.

"Do you know why we are here?" I asked Sweatt.

"No, I'm here for a meeting," he replied.

"I have a federal warrant for your arrest."

As I got to his driver side door, there were several other investigators around me.

"Exit your vehicle and place your hands behind your back," I told him, and he complied.

As I placed him in handcuffs, I told him, "Once we get you searched I will tell you the reason behind all of this."

Sweatt complied with all of our requests and was then transported to a location for an interview.

I along with two others on my team remained with the vehicle while the rest of the team was directed to Sweatt's home and the KFC where he worked so that the Task Force could begin to serve search warrants and collect additional evidence.

Once search warrants arrived, investigators would begin the painstaking task of going through everything at both sites. Those of us who remained at the arrest location placed his vehicle on a tow truck and moved it to the ATF lab. The vehicle was locked in a vehicle bay and we waited until a search warrant could be obtained. Once the search warrant arrived, the three of us unlocked the vehicle and did a brief search. We knew we would come back and do a detailed search with the forensic team but were looking for anything in plain view that stood out. Chapman opened the trunk and immediately called me. "Luckett, I think I may have something here."

We were standing in a parking garage, empty of everything but this car, a work bench and a cabinet which I guessed contained forensic tools. The metal door was closed tightly and the bright lights above were doing their job nicely. When I looked in the trunk, I saw what Derek had found. A leather pouch with a hole cut out in the side and a video camcorder sticking through the hole. We left it in place and would go through it in detail when we returned. We were being requested to respond to Sweatt's apartment building to assist.

∗   ∗   ∗

In a government building surrounded by high-rise offices and bustling traffic in downtown DC, Scott, the Task Force leader, and Frank, a DC homicide detective, prepared to interview Sweatt. Before they went into the room, Scott and Frank chatted in the hall. "Frank, we're only going to get one chance at this so we have to make it good."

"I'm with you on that. How do you want to play it?"

"I'm not really sure at the moment. Let's see how he reacts to us and go from there."

"Let's do this."

For the next hour and forty-five minutes they talked with Sweatt. Initially he denied everything but listened and looked at all the evidence that had been amassed against him. Finally, he confessed to being the MD/DC/VA serial arsonist. A video camera was introduced into the interview to more effectively document his confession and the interview continued for another four hours. Thomas Sweatt confessed to setting fire to the following:

- 4 apartment buildings

- 6 vehicles

- 37 residences

- 1 attempted arson

During the execution of the search warrant on his home, investigators found seventy-five videotapes, additional Marine Corps dress pants, a Navy hat, and newspaper article about a fatal fire on Montello Street in Washington, DC which took place in 2002.

We had finally captured the serial arsonist.

I had been so busy throughout the day I had not called my wife or my boss or eaten anything. During the search of Sweatt's apartment building, one of the ATF supervisors on the scene had several pizzas delivered along with a couple cases of water and some soda. When somebody needed a break they headed to the food stash. I was numb. The enormity of what we had accomplished had not hit me yet. I grabbed a cold slice of pizza, thought it tasted like filet mignon, and called my wife.

"Hey girl, sorry I haven't called sooner."

"You ok? It's all over the news. I knew I wouldn't hear from you."

"Can you believe it? We got the guy."

"You guys have worked a long time for this, babe. Congratulations."

"We are still searching his apartment building and who knows after that. I don't have any idea when I will be home."

"Honey, you do what you have to. Just call me and update me as much as you can, ok?"

"Love you, I can't believe we have arrested this guy."

"Be safe. Call me when you can. Love you too."

When I hung up, I just sat there and looked around. People were moving all around the street which had been blocked off. There was an array of vehicles representing all the agencies present. Some with emergency lights flashing, some parked haphazardly, some with open trunks, and others parked neatly at the curb. I wondered if the way the cars were parked were representative of the people who had driven them. All of us there for the same reasons but going in a million different directions.

I savored one more slice of cold pizza heaven and headed back inside the building.

*   *   *

Now the real work began. We needed to prepare our case for trial. Review of the seventy-plus recovered tapes revealed a number of stories referencing fires set by the serial arsonist over the past two years. They also revealed a number of military personnel in uniform and Metro Transit drivers in uniform unknowingly being recorded. They showed men in uniform from sporting events and from the military. Everyday was a learning experience. We started to see the things the arsonist enjoyed. A room had been set up to watch the tapes. It wasn't a room, just a closet, but it worked fine. A tape player, shelving to hold the tapes, a TV monitor, and a couple chairs. Like everything else we had done over the last two years, supervisors took their turn viewing the craziness he had recorded. At some point on most days the room was filled beyond capacity because something had been found on a tape that was creepy or unreal, like footage of some guy driving a bus. What made it strange was the footage was taken from behind the driver. It was recording his butt moving in the seat as he drove and then showing his large feet as they worked the pedals. Every night as I drove home, I was left to my own thoughts. I tried to figure out what made this man think the way he did. What made him enjoy the kinds of things he enjoyed. I wanted to talk to him.

On May 10, 2005, just fourteen days after his arrest and confession, Thomas Anthony Sweatt signed a plea agreement, pleading guilty to the following:

- Five counts of arson of a building used in interstate commerce;

- Two counts of use of a firearm during a crime of violence;

- Six counts of possession of an unregistered firearm;

- One count of first degree murder while armed;

- One count of second degree murder while armed.

The Task Force debriefed Sweatt on six additional occasions after his plea of guilty, both in formal proffer sessions and informal ride-alongs in the affected three states. Sweatt made one request of the Task Force. He wanted to meet and talk with Chief Blackwell. He saw him on TV and said he respected him.

During this time, Sweatt provided us with information on more than 303 fires he was responsible for setting. He admitted to setting fires in the region since 1978 and said he had never been questioned about any of them until the day of his arrest. During one interview he was asked about the fire on December 20, 2003, at 5702 83rd Avenue in New Carrollton, Maryland. This was the fire that involved someone flashing their headlights at the responding engine, he was asked if he had been the driver of the vehicle that flashes its lights at the fire engines as they were responding to the scene, and later returned, turned the lights off, and then shortly turned them back on and left the area. Sweatt said he was the driver and that when the fire engines were responding he was taunting them by flashing his lights and he returned to see what was going on, but got scared and left quickly.

To date, his fires totaled 353. Sweatt continued to be cooperative with the Task Force so cases could be closed and hopefully more people could gain closure.

*   *   *

September 12, 2005 in the Federal Courthouse, in Greenbelt, Maryland, Thomas Anthony Sweatt was sentenced to two life terms plus an additional 136 years and 10 months, with no chance for parole.

In many major criminal investigations, the suspect selects a few of the investigators they trust or feel at ease speaking with. Thomas Sweatt selected Fulkerson, Daley, and I in this investigation. From the time the proffer sessions began to the day he was sentenced in federal court, Sweatt talked to us about everything he was feeling and thinking. It's unreal what people will tell you when they are really conflicted with so many things in their head. If you really listen to their words, they will begin to reveal the dark fantasies they have stored in their head. The things you hear are at times scary but if you allow them the freedom to talk, you will learn volumes about them.

On the day he was going to be sentenced, while sitting in a holding area, Sweatt had a chance to meet Chief Blackwell. They were the only people in the room. Sweatt was shackled and seated at a small table and dressed in his prison garments. He was meek, soft spoken, and apologetic. Chief Blackwell described the meeting.

"He wanted to apologize to me for what he had done," said the Chief.

Chief Blackwell told Sweatt he made it hard for a lot of people and that his December fire had interfered with his plans to take his daughter Christmas shopping. The chief did not indicate there was any return response from Sweatt. He left without shaking hands and said that the entire conversation lasted no more than five minutes.

One of the first days we rode around with Sweatt, he and I had a conversation about him.

I told Sweatt, that while I thought he was crazy and felt very strongly about the horrible things that he had done, I also understood that he was still a man who had feelings, fears, and sorrows just like everyone else.

He just listened and I continued to talk. I told him my goal was to work with him to help him heal from what he had done so that others could perhaps begin to heal as well. I wanted to learn as much from him as I could so I could use it to teach others who were in investigations. He lowered his head and said, "I'll talk to you." His voice was so soft I had to ask him to repeat himself.

"I'll talk to you," he said louder.

Some may have felt then and maybe feel now that I should not have been so friendly towards Sweatt, but I was learning a great deal and he was opening up. I wanted him to talk to me and tell me things he had kept in for a long time. If someone is trying to make someone feel safe and secure enough to speak about things that most people would not ever want to hear, they cannot judge them—just listen and try to learn. The things in the remaining chapters are what I learned by listening to Thomas Sweatt. He had designated me as one of his investigators. He trusted me and I didn't want to break that trust.

CHAPTER 15
Thomas Anthony Sweatt:
The Beginning

Thomas Anthony Sweatt is one of the most prolific arsonists of modern time. He is by far the most bizarre and dangerous of all time. He set fires all his adult life and was clever enough to never get arrested until our Task Force tracked him down and arrested him. He had one arrest for theft of jewelry from a one-night stand but the case was never prosecuted. He distinguished himself throughout his life by being a great thief, burglar, voyeur, and not getting arrested.

Thomas Sweatt was born November 1, 1954, in Roanoke Rapids, North Carolina, to Timothy Sweatt and Dozen Allen, the seventh child of eleven. The Halifax County town of 16,000 residents was just eight miles south of the Virginia-North Carolina border. Sweatt's father worked as a bank teller and as a painter; his mother worked in a school cafeteria. Sweatt grew up in the small town and began his fire setting as a teenage boy of about fifteen years old.

His first fires were brush and trash. His brothers and he would build houses in the woods out of straw, then he would burn them down and just stand by to watch and enjoy the feelings it gave him. He then graduated to slashing tires of what he described as "hot rod cars." The tire slashing was done to prevent the people from moving the car so he could "have my little time with the fire." He lived out his fantasy with the fire each time.

Sweatt moved to Washington, DC, in 1977 and began setting fires around the region in 1978. He began by setting dumpsters on fire. At first he did not have a means of transportation, but when he got a car, he moved on to other things, starting with vehicles.

SOLVING FOR X

Thomas Anthony Sweatt
(Image courtesy of the author's files)

Throughout all the years he was setting fires, he never stopped setting fire to vehicles. He began burning buildings after a failed relationship with another man. He felt it would be his way of getting revenge. If he was able to burn the home of his former lover, then he may reunite with Sweatt out of need. When this did not work, he also set the home of his ex-lover's mother on fire. Sweatt said that this not only provided him with the revenge he wanted, but he also felt a bit of power and control, something he did not have very often in his life.

Sweatt began his fire setting by pouring combustible liquid on his target. He said he became afraid of burning himself and made a change. He started to use a soda bottle or plastic quart bottle filled with a combustible liquid and then stuck a piece of cloth in the opening.

He eventually made another change, moving up to use a one-gallon jug and filling that jug with gasoline. He always filled it up and then he wove a piece of cloth through the handle for a wick. Sweatt lived a double life, never allowing anyone or anything to interfere with his fire setting. In one life, he was a hardworking man employed by the same corporation for twenty years. He started at Kentucky Fried Chicken as a dishwasher and rose to the level of store manager. He spent time at a local church doing work with groups and he could always be found working in the yard of the building owned by his sister. Sweatt always wanted the apartment building to look nice. The grass was always cut, the bushes always trimmed, and if the home next door did not look right, he would make sure he helped out to make it correct. There were people from his neighborhood and from the area where he worked that said they could not believe he was the arsonist. His visible life was always helping people.

In his other life, Thomas Sweatt would ride the streets of the DC metropolitan region stalking a target to burn. With the exception of a few short gaps, he would indulge in this habit of searching for and then fantasizing about his targets night after night for most of his adult life. Sweatt would end most of his shifts at the KFC store by giving one or more of the employees a ride home. Once that task was completed and he had met the needs of his visible life, he would begin the hunt of his dark life.

"Bob, I was always looking for the right time, the right target, and having 'the right feeling,'" Sweatt told me.

This feeling was part of his dark life, the one he never talked about to anybody. Once he trusted me and knew he could talk to me about anything it came out.

"Setting fires provided me with a chance to feel better about myself. It felt good setting fires. I was addicted to it."

"How addicted were you?" I asked.

"It was exciting and I never thought of the consequences. It gave me joy and that's all I wanted."

174

Thomas Sweatt would never set out with some particular place or thing in his mind to set on fire. He said, "It would just happen."

"Could you explain this to me?" I asked.

"I would just ride around and keep riding until it felt right. I may ride for a couple of hours before I find myself in an area that feels okay," he explained.

Once the feeling was right, he would act on it and set the fire. The feeling would change on each ride. He never went into detail about this but my belief is that it had a lot to do with what he was feeling or dealing with in his life at the time. Once the fire had been set, most of the time he would leave the area and return home. With his work complete, he could go to bed feeling good.

Sitting and talking with Sweatt, I could hardly believe he was capable of doing the horrible things he did for more than twenty-seven years. He was a well-kept man, very conscious about his appearance, always having his clothing clean and pressed. He always had a clean and freshly-shaved face and his hair was always neatly combed. He spoke very softly and never wanted to offend anyone around him. To hear him talk and be around him and not know his background, he appeared to be a very approachable and likeable man.

The first time I met and talked with him, I came away feeling some sympathy and some empathy for him. I knew what he had done, but by the second meeting and beyond, I knew he was a man who was very ill and needed a lot of help. The empathy I had for him was somewhat diminished, but it left me wanting to really have a chance at learning more about what made him tick, so I could help educate those coming behind me in the field of fire investigations. The empathy I had for him then, I still have today.

How could someone feel sorry for a person who had killed people and went around setting fires? I'm human. Sweatt is a likeable person who is sick. It's sad to think he will never get all the help he needs. If he were ever to be free in our society again, he would go directly back to setting fires and causing his terror again.

*   *   *

When I talked with him in his prison home, he told me he marveled at the roof lines he saw while riding on the prison bus from the airport and dreamed of setting those houses on fire.

I told Sweatt many times that what he was doing by being cooperative was not only helping those families he had harmed gain some type of closure, but also helping to educate those who work to catch people like himself. I never saw much of a reaction outwardly when I would tell him this, but sociopaths need to talk about themselves. It makes them feel better and makes them feel more powerful. He would talk to us whenever we wanted him to, so allowing him to do so was helpful for all of us.

With all of our modern technology, training, and experience I have wondered many times how someone could go twenty-seven years or more totally unnoticed, yet it happens everyday. In the end I can be happy that he is finally off the street. I only hope families devastated by his crimes got some closure and that Sweatt gets the help and peace he always looked for.

*   *   *

We conducted several ride-alongs with Sweatt. In the federal system, proffer sessions can be made part of a plea deal. This allows investigators to talk more with offenders and try to learn the details of their crimes. Fulkerson and Molino, the DC Homicide detective, met twice with Sweatt and his public defender. After the second visit, the lawyer said he felt there was no longer a need for him to be in the meetings. When we did a ride-along with Sweatt, we had a team of investigators go along as required by the United States Marshals Service. We would pick him up at the jail location he was being held in Southern Maryland, and go to a fast food location to provide him breakfast. He liked McDonald's or Burger King.

From there, we would head to the pre-planned jurisdiction. During ride-alongs there was always a tail car in case Sweatt decided to attempt an escape. In the main vehicle there were always at least five of us, including myself, the other supervisors, and someone from the area we had planned to ride in. At times there were more.

Task Force investigators wanted the chance to be around Sweatt because it was hard to believe the things he was telling us and the detail he provided. Sweatt indicated he had kept a scrapbook of all of his fires and kept souvenirs from every car fire he had set. He told us he had thrown these items away after he was interviewed at his business location because he did not want the authorities to find them. In fact, Sweatt told us that he had built two devices, which he had been keeping on his back porch during the month of December. He had made a New Year's resolution that he would not set any more fires and had been true to his word. No fire had been set from December 10, 2004, until his arrest on April 27, 2005. Sweatt would tell us the longest time he ever went in his life without setting a fire was five years, but he never said when that was. Living in the inner city and around areas filled with low-income communities and high crime, setting a fire was easy. Sweatt never appeared out of place. An African American man in a primarily African American community, out late at night, would never draw attention.

Sweatt told us it was becoming more difficult not to set a fire, and he had moved one of the devices to his car sometime in March, but when interviewed by our investigators, he threw them away along with all his trophies and the scrapbook. "I was afraid I was going to get caught," he said.

On our first ride around, Swaett and I were seated next to each other in the back of our twelve-passenger van. These seats were ours whenever we went on a ride around. I introduced myself to him.

'Tom, I'm Bob Luckett and while we are riding around together, I'll be asking you questions. Will that be OK?"

"That will be fine," he replied.

"Do you remember me?" I asked.

"No," he replied in his mild, soft, inoffensive voice.

"I'm the guy who put you in handcuffs when you were arrested at work."

We both laughed, but his laughter had an edge as he said, "I served many officers at my restaurant. You all would come and when I put the food on your table, I always felt I knew you and knew you were looking for me."

I was stunned, immediately drawn to the fact of how close we were to him, and it felt like an earthquake.

"I dreamed about you, Tom, not of you per se, but of catching and arresting the serial arsonist."

Sweatt quietly laughed.

"That's all behind us now," I said. "We're just guys talking, riding around and talking. Hopefully learning from you about the stuff you did."

Sweatt was quiet but I could tell he was digesting what I had said. I wondered if he was calculating his next comment or just soaking in the power I was bestowing upon him.

On one of our rides in September 2005, Sweatt had us drive all over DC, from one side to the other. He gave us information and details on many fires we had never discovered. We were going by places I had never even heard of. In the end, we were informed about fourteen residential fires, twenty-seven vehicle fires, and three commercial building fires, for a total of forty-four. These fires went as far back as 1984 and included injuries to both firefighters and civilians. What I found so interesting, as did all of the people who had a chance to ride with him, was the recall he was able to provide. The intimate details only the person who had set the fires would know.

He told us of a fire he set in 2003 on Alabama Avenue, Southeast DC. These were residential locations under construction at the time. He had placed his device in the basement in the early morning hours. The media coverage was extensive and he recalled that one firefighter had fallen through the floor in the basement and newspaper accounts blamed poor construction.

"I could only laugh."

He seemed proud that they were wrong and his work was "good" and he finished by saying "that fire burned for a long time."

A review of the incident report indicated it was a long burning fire. Playing to his importance, I said, "Did you know the President of the United States only has a five-person security detail. You have a minimum of seven most of the time. You're more important than the President of the United States in that way."

Sweatt smiled; he clearly enjoyed being more important than someone after a life of solitude and unhappiness but he didn't respond to the comment directly. As the group rode through the streets of DC much like he had done for years, he told us about a fire he had set in the 1984 to 1986 time frame.

"This fire was in an apartment building. I entered the building and went to the lower level where I saw a large pair of work boots sitting by a door. I poured gasoline and lit the fire," he said.

There was complete silence in the van. Each one of us listened to his every word.

"It was one or two in the morning." He said that he was driving his sister's car, a maroon Chevrolet Camaro. He had left the scene and then came back. He parked and went into the crowd.

"I heard many people talking about it," he said.

This fire was truly an indication to me on how he was selecting targets. He was walking the halls of an apartment building. He saw a pair of large work boots and that was enough for him to create a fantasy and set the building on fire.

On another day when riding in Prince George's County, Sweatt took us to a townhouse development in the Oxon Hill area. When we entered the complex he said, "This looks a lot different than the way I remember it. When I burned this place it was under construction. I set a row of townhouses on fire that sat on the right hand side of the street. The flames got so big and a wind was blowing so hard that it caused the fire to catch a row of houses across the street from the original row on fire. The fire was so big, it caused a gas pipe to explode."

Whenever Sweatt was telling us about one of his jobs, nobody spoke. The air in the van always became thick with anticipation. Each of us wondering and waiting what he was going to say next. While he was telling this story, an investigator with PG fire was researching the call on a laptop computer to see if he could determine if what he was telling us was true. He never spoke; he just listened.

"Thomas, can you tell us when this fire was?" I asked.

His response was almost immediate, "2001."

"Do you remember when you set it?"

"It was in the wintertime and was very cold."

"Do you remember what time it was?"

"About two in the morning," he said.

Then he became very quiet. After a few minutes he said, "I'm sorry, I told you an incorrect time. I did not set the fire at two in the morning but five in the morning."

The investigator from PG finally spoke up and said, "You are correct, that fire came in at 0450 hours."

Sweatt said nothing, but all of us were looking at each other in disbelief.

As we continued our rides, Sweatt would insert himself in the friendly banter taking place among the investigators. At one point Daley asked Sweatt, "Have you ever set a church on fire?" and went on to indicate a particular location where a church had been set on fire.

Sweatt replied, "No, I do not set churches on fire."

Everyone laughed.

"That wasn't an unreasonable question. You have been setting fires for over twenty years and it was easy to think that you may have set just about everything on fire including churches," I said.

"I don't do churches." He had made his point and he had brought humor into the conversation.

This process, which would seem odd or perhaps even unnecessary to some, was vital to being accepted by Sweatt. He was a man with a need to be needed and wanted to feel a part of something. Being a part of our wisecracking and conversations made him feel accepted, safe, and part of our fraternity. It was important for him to feel a part of everything. Sweatt told us he appreciated not being judged, and that made him feel at ease with all of us.

One afternoon we stopped for a snack and drinks. "Thomas, you want a drink?" Hoglander asked.

"A Pepsi," he replied.

After he was given the drink, he made a remark, "I can not remember the last time I had a cold soda in a bottle with a group of people."

I did not think much about it at first, but later in reviewing the day with others this came up. It was strange that a man fifty years old would feel so thankful that he could drink a cold drink with a group

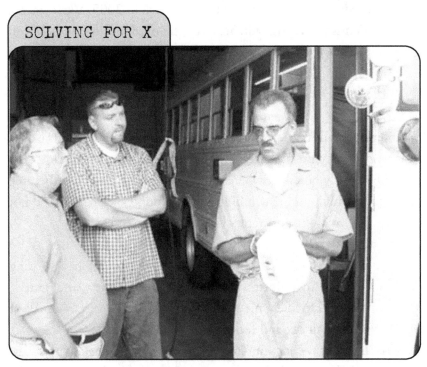

Thomas Sweatt with the author (left) demonstrating the device.
(Image courtesy of the author's files)

of guys. It made me wonder how many times in his life he had been able to just hang out with the guys and be himself.

This reinforced a valuable lesson I had learned as a young investigator many years ago. One of my mentors when I first got into fire marshal work, the man who taught me a great deal about being an investigator, taught me there is a time and place to play hardball. This simple moment in time that had absolutely nothing to do with our case investigation but everything to do with knowing people, taught me to never forget—they are people the same as us. If one can find their way past thinking about all the horrible things they have done and simply treat them as a human being, wanting to be accepted and respected just like us, it takes one a long, long way.

In fact, I think the relationships we fostered with Sweatt all those years ago would still be in place today. If we were to sit down and talk with him today it would be just like it was back in 2005. We formed a bond, a friendship, if you will. Yes, we were on opposing sides, but in the time we spent together, we were just guys doing our jobs and we did not stand in judgement of each other.

On one of our scheduled rides, I was asked to ride in the tail car, because I could have been causing Sweatt to be distracted by all the talking we were doing. Of course I agreed, but after a few hours of not seeing very many fire scenes, I was asked to switch cars and ride with him. Apparently he asked where I was a couple of times and became upset that I could not be with him. He had found a friend and did not seem to feel totally comfortable with me not around.

What motivated Thomas Sweatt to start all of these fires for so many years? Sweatt confided in us about his motives. He had a strong passion for men in uniform: military, law enforcement, firefighters, and bus drivers. He loved men with big feet, size 11 or larger. All of his fires were about sex and feeling powerful.

One incident we encountered made all of us just shake our heads. When we did our ride-arounds, we could not take him to a public restroom as he was in an orange Department of Corrections jumpsuit, handcuffed, and in waist and ankle chains. We would take him to a police station or fire house and escort him in and out. We visited a fire station in Virginia one day and had to walk through the locker room to get him to the bathroom. As we were leaving, Sweatt stopped and made a comment about a pair of shoes sitting on the floor and only partly showing.

"It sure would be nice to have some fun with those." We all laughed and kept him moving outside.

"What would be so great about those shoes?" I asked.

"Oh, they were shoes who belonged to a man with very large feet," was his reply.

"Now how would you know that? You could only see part of the back end of the shoes?"

Sweattt just smiled and said, "Oh! I can tell big-footed shoes when I see them."

There were some uncomfortable laughs as we went to the van. Before we left the parking lot, I ran back in to thank the station officer for allowing us to use the facilities and went back to the locker room. I just had to know. The shoes were size thirteen. Guess he could tell. Nothing was said until we had taken him back to his housing facility, and when we were reviewing the events of the day, I told them the shoes he had marveled at were in fact size thirteen.

Laughing and shaking our heads was the best any of us could do.

Thomas Sweatt is a unique person in the history of setting fires because of several factors. First he is African American; most fire setters are white. He began setting fires at the age of fourteen or fifteen and continued to set them until his arrest at age fifty. There is no record that he was ever interviewed by any fire investigators, nor did he have any involvement with any type of educational program focused on fire. These programs are often provided to kids who have been found setting fires at a young age, teaching them about the dangers of fire, how much damage they can cause, and trying to discourage them from playing with fire again.

Finally, the thing that may make him the most unique is that he is a paraphilia pyromaniac. In other words, every fire that he set, he set for sexual gratification.

Pyrophilia is a sexual perversion in which the person derives gratification from some odd fettish, in this case fire and fire-starting activity. It distinguishes itself from pyromania by the person's gratification being sexual in nature. I have been in public service more than forty years, and Sweatt is the only one I have ever encountered. They are very, very rare.

Until recently, his motives could not be discussed. An agreement at the time of his arrest made with his public defender and the United States Attorney's Office, prohibited any public discussion of his motives and history. They could only be discussed openly in a classroom setting while instructing other investigators.

Sweatt changed all that by corresponding over a year's time with a freelance writer named Dave Jamison, who wrote an article that appeared in *The City Paper* in Washington, DC. He also wrote letters to a volunteer firefighter named Jonathan Riffe, who penned a book about Sweatt and the things he told him. During this time Sweatt talked openly about his fire-setting history and motives.

Now I can speak freely about the information I have had since he was arrested in April of 2005. I had a close personal interaction with Sweatt. The things he told me were what I witnessed firsthand.

CHAPTER 16
Thomas Anthony Sweatt: Conversations

Sweatt began setting fires in his boyhood hometown of Roanoke Rapids, North Carolina. He started with small trash fires and moved up to trash cans and dumpsters. He started having homosexual contact around age 14 and found that he enjoyed masturbation as a form of sexual release.

He also discovered he enjoyed creating fantasies prior to setting his fires. He told me that in his teen years he found cars sexy, something he enjoyed all of his life. In the 60s and 70s, the cars he liked were called street rods or hot rods. He would slash the tires of the cars so they could not be moved and then he would have his little time with fire. He would build a fantasy in his mind about the vehicle. These fantasies were never fully described to me by Sweatt, but involved a sexual nature with the car and or the driver and then he would set fire and masturbate to complete the fantasy.

After moving to Washington, DC, he obtained his own car, and he would ride around until he felt comfortable in an area. What it took to make him feel comfortable was never the same. Sometimes it would be the neighborhood; sometimes it would be someone he saw. It might be how a place looked and when he felt it, he then set a fire. Again, his fire setting in the beginning was small stuff: trash, wood, paper, dumpsters, and general household items.

We talked about the incident involving his boyfriend.

"Bob, when we broke up I was devastated. I didn't know what to do. I had never had a real boyfriend before. Most of my flings were one-night stands."

"I'm sure you were hurting," I said.

"He wouldn't even talk to me. I got mad."

I just listened and tried to show him through my attention that I cared.

"I wanted revenge for him treating me that way. Things didn't really go like I had planned though."

"What happened?" I asked.

"I thought if I burned his home, he would come running out and I would be there to save him. I would wrap my arms around him and he would know he was safe with me."

"That didn't happen?"

"No, it didn't. He never spoke to me."

"Sorry Thomas," I said.

"I decided I would set his mother's house on fire and knew that he would come back to me for sure then."

"Did he come back?"

Sweatt dropped his head, got quiet for a minute, and then softly said, "Nothing worked; he never spoke to me again."

"I'm sorry, you must have been upset for some time. I know I would have been."

"I was for a bit, but something happened to me during that time that really changed things."

"What happened?"

"I felt happiness, excitement, and fulfillment when I set those fires," he replied.

I wasn't sure I was hearing him correctly and wanted to make sure he knew I was listening to him. He needed to know I felt what he was saying was important.

"Thomas, I want to make sure I understand what you were saying. When you set those two homes on fire you felt excitement, happiness, and fulfillment?"

"Sounds crazy doesn't it?" he said. "I really enjoyed it. I felt powerful. I was content when I set a fire and saw the results of my work. I could set anything I wanted on fire."

He in fact did just that for the next 20-plus years. He set cars on fire. He set commercial buildings on fire. He would set fires in hallways of buildings. He would set construction sites on fire and he would set occupied homes on fire.

There did not seem to be any pattern to why he would set something on fire. Sweatt indicated he would just get in his car and drive around. These drives could last a couple of hours or more before he would get a feeling of comfort.

When he finally felt comfortable in a neighborhood, he would select a target. He would then approach it and, at times, just sit in front of it, or perhaps look in the windows at the people inside or go on to their porch or deck and just sit. While sitting there he would create a fantasy about the location, like it was his.

In looking at the many homes Sweatt had set on fire, they all seemed to have many things in common. I asked him about this. "Thomas, the overall look of the buildings you burned were similar: simple and neat, they all had siding."

"Siding burns easier," Sweatt said.

"They all seemed to be near a park or school," I said.

"This often provided an easy means of escape," he said.

"I didn't have a particular place in mind when I went out at night, I just wanted to feel comfortable, like I was home."

All the single family homes he burned seemed to have these similar features. A person likes what they like and while maybe not in their conscious mind, it still affects what they do.

One of the fires he set was at 2800 Evarts Street, in Washington, DC. Sweatt was drawn to the location because he had seen the grandson of the owner enter and exit from there.

Thomas said, "The guy was attractive looking." When he made the decision to set the house on fire, it was not to harm the owner or her grandson, but instead to have the grandson, whom he had been fantasizing about come running out and into his arms so he could help him. He hoped this would lead to a relationship with him. Sweatt

187

SOLVING FOR X

2800 Evarts Street
(Image courtesy of the author's files)

indicated that he sat on the front porch for forty-five minutes before he set the house on fire. He said he was just enjoying the wonderful garden the home had and just wanted to be a normal person and have a home and garden like that.

In talking with Sweatt, he never thought about the people he was hurting or the damage he was doing. He said he only wanted to feel better about himself and setting fires was the only time he felt good. He never thought about getting caught and really never thought he would get caught. Sweatt lived his life as though he was being watched and followed all the time. He could teach a countersurveillance course to anyone by teaching them how he lived. As the time approached that we were going to arrest him, he was under surveillance twenty-four hours a day. I was just amazed at the things I saw him do.

We were following him in lunch time traffic in downtown DC, and he would drive two blocks in one direction and then in the middle of a traffic line, he would pull out and make a U-turn and go back in the opposite direction. He did this type of thing all the time and later confirmed it. There was not a day we followed him that he did not lose us for a short period of time. I was fully convinced that we had been made and discussed several times with others that we needed to take him sooner than we did because of this fact. Once he was arrested and we were able to talk with him, Sweatt said he never had any idea we were following him and never had a sense that anyone was around him until I cut him off leaving the parking lot and placed him under arrest. He told us that was just his way of life and always did those kinds of things so he would never get caught. I found this odd at first, but as I spent more time talking with him, I learned some of the reasons he did things this way.

Riding with us through Prince George's County, Sweatt directed us to an area of single family homes. As we were riding down the street he told us to stop at a particular house, one we had never been to prior. It was a single family home with a metal carport. Sweatt told us he had attempted to set this place on fire. He had parked his car about a half a block away and walked up to a vehicle parked under the carport. He went to the rear of the car and before he could do anything a voice came out of the window behind him and told him if he did not get his ass out of there he would be killed.

"It was a warm night and the window was open."

While this may not seem like anything spectacularly revealing, it showed me that Sweatt really did not have any fear about being caught. If the feeling was right, he acted on it. With the window being open and the possibility of being caught so great, I would think he would have just moved on, but he didn't until he was told he would be killed.

If it had not been for some man inside that house, sleeping near that window and hearing him, Sweatt would have burned the car. As we were about to leave this location, Sweatt told us of another location he had set on fire.

"Go to the next block and turn right. As soon as you turn there will be a red Ford Mustang parked in the driveway," Sweatt said.

We drove the one block and made the right as he had directed us, and there, sitting in the driveway was a red Ford Mustang.

"Thomas, what made you select that location?" Scott asked.

"I had seen that vehicle and the person driving it on the road. I liked it and just followed the vehicle home."

"When did you do this?" I asked.

"It was in 2000."

This event had taken place almost five years previous and he was able to talk about it like it happened yesterday. What made it even more crazy was the fact he could not have known that after he had burned the car the replacement would have been the same.

I believe that each and every fire event was significant to the life of Thomas Sweatt and I believe this was why he was able to recall so much about each one. The events of a particular fire were etched into his memory and he would always recall and enjoy each and every one of them. They each held a special place within him and he needed to hold on to their memory. He needed relationships and did not have them. He had a sexual fantasy with every fire; he masturbated during and sometimes after each fire and they became special moments to him.

He recalled each one because he gave himself to each just like we do in our human relationships. Sweatt's relationships were with the fires.

Strange as it is, every fire he set became a sexual experience and he cherished each one.

During one of our ride-alongs, we were riding in Arlington County, Virginia, and Sweatt took us to a Metro drivers' parking lot. The location is across the street from a Metro bus barn and in an area of great activity, with shops and stores all around. Sweatt told us he had followed a driver there one night after getting off from work and then driving around.

He saw the guy park his car and then cross the street to the yard where he picked up his bus and began his route. He saw the guy come out driving his bus and followed him for a bit. He said he knew he would not be able to do anything with the driver so he went back to the lot where the guy had parked. He parked again and sat there for a long time.

"How long did you sit there?" I asked.

"At least a few hours," he said. "I saw a shop on the backside of the parking lot and thought about setting that on fire, but changed my mind and decided on the vehicle that I had seen the driver bring into the lot. It was the middle of the afternoon and I just walked over to the car near a front wheel well, and I placed a jug and set it on fire."

He was not boasting or saying it was something special. He was just flatly explaining what he did and how he did it. No big deal.

We drove past several residential parking lots in our ride-alongs and Sweatt would often boast that the chain link fencing placed around the lots were put there as a direct result of his work.

"Fellas, that fence is a Thomas Sweatt fence."

This became a calling card of sorts for him. We would see a location and tease him with something like, "Is this more Thomas Sweatt fence?"

Everyone would give that laugh that is both disgusting and funny and he would simply reply, "Yes."

We would go by a commercial location and Sweatt would take us to the rear of a building and show us where the building still showed scars of his work with blackened brick or boards still in a spot where a window had once been. Again, this was never boasting or grandstanding. He was just showing us where he had done his work. We would just ride and he would tell us to go here or go there. We always had investigators from the area we were riding in and we had a list of unsolved fires that we hoped Sweatt would admit to.

When we took him to Alexandria, Virginia, which is where I worked, he said he did not come here very often.

"Why?" I asked.

"There is too much brick," he said.

"Why didn't you ever seem to go to Georgetown?" Georgetown is an area of Washington known as a trendy area with high-dollar homes, many nightspots, and food establishments.

"I never went there and set any fires because they could build a new house the next day."

This seemed strange to us because one might think that a person who came from meager means would more than likely direct their actions toward those who had a lot. This did not fit for Sweatt because he looked at his victims differently.

"I wanted them to need me and if I couldn't have them I really didn't want anyone else to have them."

Sweatt was simply looking for ways to establish what he called a normal life. He wanted to be in a relationship with someone, wanted a regular home, and wanted all the things that went with that. In this sense he was very much like most of us. He wanted someone to be with. He wanted his life to have some structure and to him, this was normal, but something he never seemed able to achieve. Sweatt never thought about the pain and suffering he was putting others through because by setting the fires he was eliminating his own pain and suffering.

Sweatt told me before his arrest he had a desire to move out of the city and was waiting for his sister to retire from her job with the phone company. I asked him if he had someplace in mind to go. "We really didn't, but we knew we wanted to go to the country," he said. There had been several rides looking at the pretty homes to figure it out, but they never really decided.

I wondered if his decision might be based on places he thought might look good setting on fire. These types of thoughts never seemed to be too far from his mind.

Thomas Sweatt had not set a fire since December 10, 2004 and it was now May of 2005, but his desire to set one was just as great as it ever was. He missed his fires and talked about one of his biggest desires: he wanted to set a Metro bus driver on fire.

"I have thought about this often since I made the resolution to stop setting fires. I knew when I started again I was going to need something a little more exciting," he said.

He had never acted upon these thoughts in the past because he could not figure out how to get on the bus, set the driver on fire, and get himself out safely.

I had always been taught that an arsonist will always want to escalate their fire setting behavior. These thoughts and comments confirmed that. We had seen him make many types of changes in the two years we tracked him, and now he was confiding in us about what his next escalation would have been. If he had acted on these thoughts and was successful at taking a life when he was actually trying to take one, how much additional empowerment would he have felt? How many more times would he have tried to burn someone before we caught him?

Sweatt loved men in uniform, but he loved what he called "sexy cars" even more. In our conversations, Sweatt came to know that I was a member of the 1971 TC Williams Titans high school football team, made famous in the Disney movie *Remember the Titans*, starring Denzel Washington. He knew I had a picture of Mr. Washington in my home and he found this very exciting. He has asked for a copy of that picture more than once.

One day I asked him, "Tom if you could have your choice of being with Denzel Washington in a Marine Corps dress uniform or being with a tricked out SUV, like a Denali, with 18-inch tires, chromed-out spinners, chromed grill, leather interior, and large sound system, and shiny black paint, which would you choose?"

Sweatt did not even have to think and provided me with his answer in almost a single instant.

"Bob, I would take the SUV every time."

"Why?"

"I would take the SUV because after I had made love to it, I could burn it."

Simple and to the point. A little better insight on a man that loved fire and how all his dealings with fire involved sex and or a sexual fantasy.

In November of 2018, I sent a letter to Sweatt at the Federal Prison Facility he was at in Petersburg, Virginia. I wanted to let him know I was writing this book. He responded back to me rather quickly. He admitted that when the letter arrived he did not recognize the name and just thought it was somebody writing to him to inquire about his fires. Once he started reading it he remembered me.

"You made my day," he wrote. "Wow it has been a long time and it just seems like yesterday when you and Scott would come and get me at Charles County to drive around looking at various fires. Odd as it might seem, we had fun and you were always cracking jokes. You made me feel comfortable all the time," he said in his letter back to me.

"Bob, I'm excited to learn that you are writing a book about the investigation into the arson case. If you ever get it published, would you send me a copy? Many times the inmates here would come up to me and say, 'Tom I saw you on TV last night.' I've yet to see it. There have been several DC detectives come here to interview me about more fires. Some were mine, some were not.

"I still love fires. I still love the military and I still love fire trucks and engines. I still love police cruisers (especially DC) and would it be too much to ask if you'd send me some pictures of firemen and fire trucks to look at?"

Thomas Anthony Sweatt is in prison for the rest of his life but he is still thinking about setting fires and all the things he loved to set on fire.

Thomas Anthony Sweatt is truly one of the rarest serial arsonists of all time. The other serial arsonists I discussed in this book are who I think rival him. One could argue that only one of them can be number one, but I will give Thomas Sweatt that #1 rating every time.

He used a vehicle, he set occupied family homes on fire, and he carried the pieces of his device with him so he could build one when he found the right target. While his device was not very sophisticated, it was highly reliable and allowed for his quick exit before fully igniting. He was a genius at hiding his intent. He walked along in the community carrying his device and people just thought he was a guy carrying his groceries. He was a black man striking in mainly black neighborhoods. He was openly gay. He was a lifelong voyeur who loved to secretly video people and use them to build his fantasy. He was a very goal-oriented arsonist: the goal being to have his victim need his love.

He sets himself above the rest in being unique. This also makes him very dangerous. He used sexual motivation as his primary thought in every fire and it provided him with great power and thrills.

Thomas Anthony Sweatt

- Black Male

- 50 years of age

- Loner

- Unable to maintain relationships

- Father was very strict

In the end, this is what Sweatt's reign of terror produced:

- 4 known deaths

- Several injuries to citizens and firefighters

- Fire setting history covering 27 plus years

- 353 known set fires

- Millions of dollars in damage

CHAPTER 17

Thomas Anthony Sweatt: Trying to Understand

I wanted to have a better understanding of how Sweatt lived and operated. When we searched his vehicle, we found a black leather case that had a hole cut into the side and I asked about this.

"I enjoyed videotaping people or things that I liked and found sexy. I would use the tapes to create my own form of personal pornography. They helped me create my sexual fantasies so I could masturbate."

Thomas Sweatt would masturbate several times a day. He would ride around and see someone walking, he would then turn around and get on the other side of the street and videotape them. He would follow until they stopped someplace like a bus stop. He would continue to tape them and start constructing a fantasy in his mind. Sometimes these taping sessions would last an hour or more, until his target left the area. He told us of a time he was riding around in Washington, DC, and heard a sexy voice. He rode past a group of young men several times until he was able to figure out who's voice he had noticed.

He then parked and began to tape the young man and the group. He got out with his leather briefcase slung over his shoulder and walked past this group, taping all the time.

"Why did you do that?" I asked

"I wanted to get a closer look at the sexy-voiced stranger. I taped them until the group broke up and the sexy guy went into a building. I allowed some time to pass and entered the building to get some more footage."

"So what did you do with the tape?"

"My fantasy was complete. I just needed to set the building on fire and wait for my man to escape and come to me."

Sweatt then sat in his car and allowed the events of the fire to unfold, masturbating the entire time. He would become so good at making these fantasies and they would excite him so much that he said he could climax and never touch himself.

I asked Thomas to give me more details about these fantasies.

"When I saw someone I liked I would begin to think about establishing a relationship with them," he said.

Despite the fact that Sweatt never had any lasting relationships in his adult life, he told us he had several one-night stands. He was never really close to anyone. When he would feel himself getting close to someone, he would back away. He said this was because he was never really close to his family and never felt loved by either of his parents. He was close to his mother, but not his very strict father. Sweatt wanted to be needed by his victims and he needed them. When he would set their home or car on fire, the fantasy would continue with the person escaping the fire and he would be there to comfort them. Sweatt hoped they would become lovers.

In the end, the fire would be his "savior" because if he could not have this person, then he really did not want anyone to have this person. Any other victims caught up in his fires were just collateral damage. He was just worried about his target and feeding his sexual desires.

I was beginning to understand why and how his recall of all of these fire events was so good. Each fire represented someone he had a sexual experience with, and since he was unable to sustain a relationship with any real person, he did it through his fantasy process.

I will never forget one sexual experience he told us about that involved a firefighter who lived in one of the apartments in the building Sweatt's sister owned. Having a firefighter living above him became so wonderful in his mind that he had to act on it.

Sweatt would often do maintenance in many of the units to keep costs down and as such had a pass key. He entered this firefighter's apartment and after searching around he found a pair of fire boots. These boots are a type often worn by firefighters. They are all leather, about 12-inches high, with a steel toe, and a zipper built into the laces. The boots are very heavy and at times very uncomfortable to wear. Sweatt reminded us that he liked men with big feet, size 11 or greater. He said that he took these boots back to his apartment and placed them on the stove. He turned the stove on and waited until the bottoms of the boots began to burn and smoke. He loved the smell of leather burning. When the boots reached this point, he removed them and took them to bed and made love to them. When he was finished making love to them he took them back to the owner's apartment. This firefighter was his and he did not want anyone moving in on his territory, so he masturbated in all the corners of the firefighter's apartment.

He said, "This firefighter belonged to Thomas Sweatt."

Sweatt loved military recruiters and he loved to talk with them. He developed a process where he would call and tell them he had a son or a nephew getting ready to graduate from high school and was thinking about enlisting. He would get them to come to his apartment to gather additional information. When they would arrive he would tell them his nephew was not home from work yet and would engage in casual conversation until he felt comfortable.

Then he would move in and sit directly next to them and at some point just reach over and grab this recruiter's crotch.

This was so far-fetched I would have not believed it had I not seen it with my own eyes when I spent my time in the video closet watching the video tapes we had collected from his home. It was hard for me to understand why none of the recruiters ever reported contact with him. I guess if I was a young Marine I would not tell anybody back in the office that some guy just reached out and grabbed my crotch.

Sweatt said he called these recruiters over four hundred times. We were unable to confirm this, but I can tell you that most of the recruiting stations around the Washington, DC Metro region had been visited by Thomas Sweatt, and while they did not know him on a personal basis, they knew who he was.

He had stolen from recruiter's unlocked cars; he had visited recruiting sites only to go in a restroom and masturbate or just sit in the parking lot and video the men in uniform. He had burned something at just about all of these recruiting stations as well. Toward the end of our investigation, several area recruiting locations were hit by fire.

When we arrested Sweatt, he confessed to all of the incidents and confirmed this by providing intimate details of the events. This also showed he never really stopped setting fires.

I asked Sweatt about these four hundred-plus calls and home visits. I wanted to know why he called them.

His answer was simple. "To have sex."

"How many times have you been successful in having sex with these men?"

Again, his answer was simple. "Zero."

OK, now I was really confused. "If you called them to get them to come over to have sex and you never accomplished this, then why would you keep calling?"

He explained that he called all the time because he loved to videotape them while they were in his home. The recruiters never knew they were being filmed but Sweatt did it every time. He had a reason for grabbing their crotch. "I was trying to shock them. I wanted them to be so angry that they would fight me."

When they reacted and hit him, he would hug them, touch them all over, and kiss them while they were punching him and calling him dirty names. "I loved to hear the sound of grappling with the men when I watched the tapes. When they would finally leave I would play the tapes over and over in slow motion and masturbate. I looked forward to these occasions very much, they were my sexual release."

When the recruiters would not fight with him, he felt he would become more sexually frustrated and this would cause him to offend and set another fire. He had stolen enough items from recruiter vehicles that he was able to construct what he called "a Marine dress uniform." He had a dress cap, dress shirt, and dress pants. He used to put the clothes on and stand in front of the mirror and try to talk in a more rugged fashion. He would practice walking the way he thought a Marine should walk. He would video these sessions and use them to masturbate. He would neatly iron the entire uniform then place it on the bed lying it flat. He would then have sex with the uniform. He had wanted to be a Marine but failed, now he was able to have sex with one whenever he wanted.

Sweatt knew the phone numbers to every fire station in Washington, DC. He said he went through periods of time, which he identified as "fads," when he would call every fire station every night just to hear the voices of the firemen.

He knew which ones had the nice guys and which ones did not. When he would call, he would talk dirty to whomever answered the phone in hopes of getting them to talk dirty back.

He said he would tell them things like, "I'm hot and need a sexy black fireman to put my fire out." He would at times say he was looking for tall, sexy firefighters to come rescue him. Some of the stations would talk back to him and some would just hang up. But there were some, Sweatt said, "who would say mean things to me. The ones that talked mean had to pay."

He said he went to one station and burned four personal vehicles in the lot in one night. We confirmed that there was a station where multiple vehicles burned but cannot confirm it was Sweatt's work.

The theme of people being nice to him played out in all of his little ventures. If he called or visited a recruiting office and they talked mean to him or treated him poorly, they paid. He felt he was not hurting anyone by talking dirty or masturbating in a restroom and they should not treat him badly for being who he was.

One afternoon he was ticketed by a DC Metropolitan police officer for parking in a handicap space outside a Safeway grocery store. The next evening he saw this officer again and followed him for hours while the officer was on patrol and responding to calls. Finally the officer returned to his precinct station, pulled his cruiser in the fenced lot, and went inside. Sweatt allowed some period of time to pass to make sure the officer was not coming directly back, and then he struck. He entered the fenced parking lot, found the cruiser, and used one of his devices to set the car on fire. He returned to his car and watched the events of the fire unfold.

During his reign of terror in the DC area, Sweatt burned eight marked police cruisers and four unmarked cars. He said that he loved policemen in uniform but at the same time disliked the authority they represented or used toward him. There was nothing that Sweatt would not or could not burn if he put his mind to it. He did have limitations, it seems, as he told us he would not burn a church.

In all of our conversations, there was only one time I really got upset and just wanted to punch him in the face or choke the hell out of him. Those were my emotions associated with the events of September 11, 2001, and what happened to the 343 firefighters who died in New York and all those who died at the Pentagon and in Pennsylvania. Looking back, I don't think he was actually trying to provoke me or anyone in the room at the time in any way. He was simply having a conversation.

We were returning from a ride-around trip and I asked, "Tom, I'm curious to know if the events associated with that day had affected you in setting any fires."

"Seeing the Pentagon burn did not really affect me," Sweatt said, but added that he did ride the subway over to the Pentagon and looked at the site a couple of times, and then rode the trains and watched the people, but it did not cause him to set any more fires. The only thing I enjoyed or that affected me in any way was all the firemen's funerals. I really enjoyed seeing all those men in their dress uniforms and standing at attention."

When he said this we were sitting in the parking lot of his

Southern Maryland jail facility. We usually chatted for a while before he was taken back inside. When those words left his mouth, there was complete silence. I felt every eye in the van on me and I was burning. I really just wanted to choke him for saying that. Thank goodness I did nothing. In fact, I cannot tell you what I did other than change the subject. Had I shown my temper to him, it more then likely would have ended our friendship, or at least changed it. I had never shown any judgemental emotions about anything he told me about his actions or his thoughts. I could not show him any now. When he got out of the van, the words that flowed from all of us were those of angry people needing to vent. Looking back at it now, I know it was purely an emotional reaction from all of us.

Prior to getting out of the van, Sweatt talked at length about how much he loved firemen and seeing them daily on television in their dress uniforms and he meant nothing more. Nonetheless, the 343 who died should never be forgotten and never be talked about in any negative or disrespectful fashion. When someone speaks about them at all, there will always be emotion from me.

Talking with Sweatt was a study of all the things you learn in interviewing school. This man could be recorded for several hours and then you could use that to teach an entire class on the subject of interviewing. Let me try to explain.

Each time we would pick him up to conduct a ride, he and I would sit together. He began every ride the same way. He would begin a bit standoffish, waiting to see what I had to say or had to offer and then decide how he would react, which is fairly typical suspect-type behavior. Working with him, I learned quickly that he listened to every word said, and he quickly factored what was wanted. If a speaker did not listen carefully to what he was saying, they would miss some meaning hidden in the words. He truly kept the importance of listening to him in the front of my mind. When Scott and the homicide detective from DC interviewed him on the day he was arrested, they never raised their voices or became confrontational. They just had a

SOLVING FOR X

United States Penitentiary in Terre Haute, Indiana
Public Domain Image

man-to-man conversation that lasted several hours. The talk was very matter-of-fact and Sweatt responded in the same fashion. I took my lead from them and each and every time we were together we were just going to have a good old fashioned conversation, getting to know each other and talk.

We maintained this process anytime we talked with him. The two federal agents who ran the investigation and I flew from Baltimore to Indiana so we could debrief him again. We were there to meet with Sweatt, who was now inmate #38792037, in the federal prison in Terre Haute, Indiana. We were hoping to find out if there was anything additional Sweatt had to tell us that we had not covered in our ride-arounds with him before he was transferred there from Southern Maryland.

There was a period of time while we were there I was scared. I don't know if my partners would tell you they were, but I sure as hell was. When we arrived, we unloaded our weapons and locked them in the trunk. The only things we all seemed to be carrying when we entered the lobby were our pagers.

"Sorry, no entry allowed!" a rather large corrections officer informed us as we walked in the front door. "Please return to your vehicle and remove everything from your pockets and person and return."

We had to get permission to bring in our notebooks and pens. I was getting a bit nervous.

Upon our return, we were allowed to pass about a hundred feet farther from the lobby where we encountered a bulletproof window with bars. There were more corrections officers waiting for us there. We were instructed to sign a couple of documents. I didn't read them fully but it was telling us we would be recorded and videotaped while we were there. With that completed, a large, steel, gray door opened and we walked through. That earned us another ten feet into the facility. It was like being a rat in a cage, having to complete one task before getting a treat. When the very large door closed behind us, another in front of us opened and we moved another ten feet into a glass cube. Just the sounds of these extra heavy metal doors opening and closing was enough to make you a bit uneasy. While in the glass cube, we were met by the corrections officer who would be our guide and take us to our meeting with Sweatt. Officer Edwards was a nice guy doing his job. No fanfare here, just business.

Another heavy metal door opened and officer Edwards simply said, "This way." As he began to walk down a hall, he said, "Gentlemen, keep your right shoulders toward the wall."he said.

There was a big, wide yellow stripe on the wall to remind everyone where their right shoulder should be.

I felt like I better get with the program and not ask any questions. There was not much talk between the four of us. We did not have to go far to our meeting room. When we entered, there were a few chairs, a desk, a phone, and a bank of windows so everything that happened in the room could be seen from the outside. Sweatt was escorted in by another officer who left quickly. We did our greetings and then moved into a smaller room off to the side to conduct our interview. Sweatt appeared happy to see us and after a couple of minutes of chit-chat, we got down to asking questions.

Shortly after our meeting started, the lights in our room went out. Sitting in the pitch-black darkness of a small unfamiliar room makes one a bit uncomfortable or even a little unsure of what was going on, like a child scared of the dark. I was scared of the dark as a child and still reach my hand first in a dark room and turn the lights on before I entered. Learned habits.

This room of total darkness was in a federal prison which housed some of the most serious criminals in the country, like Timothy McVay, the Oklahoma City bomber. I'm sitting less than two feet from a convicted serial arsonist murderer, who wants to be back out in the free world setting fires again. I cannot see anything, only hear and feel the warm breath of this killer, smelling the onions he had at his last meal. The only true way for me to know that this guy is still in his chair is to reach out and touch him and that simply was not going to happen. My partners were sitting just across the table from us. After what seemed like an eternity, Officer Edwards approached the door leading to the outer office and slowly opened it.

In complete darkness, I heard the door moan and creak while he opened it, then heard him quietly say, "Well this is not good."

Sweatt said nothing; we all sighed but said nothing.

I discovered that when your federal prison corrections officer guide says, "Things are not good," your mouth gets dry real quick. Officer Edwards seemed to take it all in stride. He made his way to a phone with very slow, deliberate movements and made a call to the main tower. The four of us were sitting in silence. The information he got back was not good either. They informed him, "the entire prison is dark and we have no idea why." He was told to keep all of us where we were.

They said, "Follow all your safety protocol and we will call back when we know more."

I'm a person who never has a problem talking and can talk to anyone, but sitting inside a maximum security federal prison with a convicted murderer, smelling the heat of his breath in the dark was not normal and the small talk did not come easy.

We did manage our way through it and when the lights came back on, we even laughed about it. The phone call that eventually came from the main tower informed us that it was a planned test to see how staff would react and nobody was told on purpose because they did not want to take a chance on the information leaking out. I would say we got a passing grade.

With that escapade behind us, we decided to do the interview in the outer room. Sweatt was placed in a chair and the three of us sat across from him. The corrections officer again stepped in and said, "This setup is not going to work. With how you have things set up, any inmates walking the hall would be able to see Sweatt."

"Okay, so what?" I asked.

"Well, you see, the other inmates would know he was in here talking with law enforcement and that would be enough to get him hurt or killed," Edwards said.

"Really?!" I said, feeling surprised.

We were able to finish our interview session without any further delays and Sweatt told us about a couple more incidents we needed to confirm.

When Sweatt was ready to return to his cell, the officer asked him, "What are you going to tell your celly?" Sweatt had not been in the place very long and the officer knew it.

Sweatt really didn't seem to know what to say. The officer wrote him out a slip and told him, "Tell your cellmate that you have been at the head doctor." Every new inmate has to see the shrink and get evaluated.

When Sweatt was gone, I asked, "Why was the note needed?"

"The celly will get the word out if there's not a believable answer," the officer said.

"Get the word out?" I asked, wondering what he meant.

"They would say he was a snitch and it would not go well for him," he said.

An experience I will never forget.

In addition to the information we gathered from Sweatt when we interviewed him in his Indiana prison, he told us more about himself.

"I was not able to be myself very much when I was with a group of men."

"Why?" Scott asked.

"They would always want to talk about sports, fixing cars, or women. I would just sit silent. I wanted to talk about gardening or cooking. I just wanted to be or feel normal. It's a shame it took me going to prison to feel free."

You have to listen to what a person is saying if you're ever going to have them open up their heart and share what's in it. Interviewing Sweatt with the typical television cop show approach of good cop-bad cop would have never worked. One had to pay attention to him all of the time and make him feel in control. He lacked this type of control in his life, and in relationships, and being the focus of attention was important to him.

Sweatt had all the body language investigators learn about. He would slump his shoulders and drop his head whenever he was about to confess something which embarrassed him. It was hard for him to talk about these things. His voice would lower even more than normal and become so low it was almost inaudible. Reassuring him often kept his confidence level up. He had an unusual tell or body tick when he had something on his mind but did not have the confidence to say. When he was building that confidence, he would always use his right hand and rub the hair on his left arm and wrist.

He would rub it like he was trying to roll it. After doing this time and time again, I asked him about it and he was totally unaware he was doing it and kept doing it without seeming to notice, even after we talked about it.

When talking with Sweatt he would become emotional at times

and begin to cry as he talked about things which bothered him. I would sit with my arm around him and just allow him to talk. I would slowly work at bringing him back to focus and then move on.

Being treated nice and being treated fair was important to Sweatt and I never wanted to lose sight of it.

After spending a few days picking him up from the Southern Maryland jail where he was first held after his arrest and riding him around, we all knew he was holding something back. The feeling was there were fires that he didn't want to talk about, fires where people were either injured or killed.

I approached those fires by telling him, "Thomas, at some point we need to get to those dark, bad fires. I won't pressure you to talk about them, but you need to know that at some point we have to talk about them. When you get back to your cell, you need to spend some time alone thinking about them so when we get on that subject it will be easier to discuss. The person who has been setting these fires for all of these years was the bad Thomas Sweatt. Part of his healing process was talking about them so he could get rid of them and heal himself."

I also told him, "Thomas, the more fires we learn about where something bad has taken place, the more people who were victims will also have a chance to heal. They need to know what really happened. Thomas, this is also important, because it is allowing us to learn more about you and how you did things as one of the best people who we have ever seen setting fires. We need as much information as we can get so we can teach others about how to catch people like you if we are faced with a similar challenge in the future."

Yes, I was playing to his ego, but more importantly, I was playing to his sense of being needed as a person and having someone wanting and needing him, and that was true.

During one of our rides, Sweatt told us to go into a part of DC that I don't think I had ever been in. We certainly had not responded to any fires in that area during our investigation. He led us to a townhouse and told us about a fire he set there in 1984 or 1985, and it had caused a death. He was sure there was a death because he had read about it in the newspaper.

"I had just left my job at Roy Rogers fast food restaurant and was walking home. I passed a guy on the street and this guy spoke to me, saying, 'Hello.' The guy was attractive and had a nice voice."

Sweatt said he allowed the man to get ahead of him so he could remain unnoticed and followed him. He followed him home and watched him enter his house.

"I was now very excited and wanted to see this guy again. I began to walk faster on my way home thinking all the time about this new fellow. This walk soon became a jog and then a run so I could get there faster."

When he finally reached his home, the excitement was so strong he said he could hardly take it. Sweatt said that he borrowed his sister's car and returned to the home where he had seen the man enter. He parked, got out of the car, and set the house on fire by pouring a flammable liquid on the porch. He then returned to his car so he could watch this man come out and, he hoped, rush into his arms. He saw the man exit looking shocked, and then he could hear screams in the house.

What Sweatt did not know was this man lived with his wife and four children: two boys and two girls. The boys got out unharmed, the girls got out from the rear, but both were burned badly. The mother, Bessie Mae Duncan, did not make it out and died from burns and smoke inhalation. The father, Roy Picott, was burned badly and died a few days later in the hospital.

Two of the children were recently contacted and informed of the new details about this fire. They did not believe it at first, having been told the fire was started by careless smoking when it took place some twenty-five years prior. Finally, they knew that their father had not caused the fire, but this man, Thomas Sweatt, who they never knew, had caused the deaths of their parents.

When we spoke with one of the daughters and told her this

information she said, "Why he did it really does not matter." She still bears the scars from Sweatt's work. "Yes," she said, "We're glad to know, but this thing happened so long ago. We really don't want to bring up all those old emotions again."

What had been done was done, their lives changed forever.

Sweatt said a few times the excitement of recording a driver on the bus would be so great he would begin to masturbate on the bus and he would get caught.

When asked what happened, he said they would either tell him to go to the back of the bus if he was going to do that or they would make him get off the bus. This made us wonder about his relationship with violence, and we asked about that. Sweatt indicated there had been a few times in his life when things got violent, but nothing ever came of them.

One time while living in an apartment, he invited a neighbor man over for dinner. After dinner, he informed the man they were going to have sex. When the man refused, Sweatt pulled out a gun. The man rushed him and they fought. Sweatt told us the man freed himself from him long enough to get out. The man later called the police who came and talked to Sweatt. He did not deny what he had done, but said even though the gun was real, it never worked and he said he showed it to the police. The police took no further action, thinking it was just a neighbor's quarrel, but they did take the gun.

Sweatt told us of a time he made a move on a Metro driver while the driver was on the bus. He grabbed the driver's crotch and then fled the bus. He said the driver chased him down and beat him up. No police were ever called.

Finally, he told us about a lover he fought with, hitting him behind the ear with some type of ax. We could never confirm this account. I believe it happened because his information on everything else he told us proved true and he had never lied to me on anything that I'm aware of.

I'm not sure how much more he has to tell, but I believe it is quite a bit. He will need the right setting with the right people, but in time, more will come out. He failed to talk about fires in the area from 1978 to 1984. I hope someone, maybe even me, can be there when he does decide to talk.

In November 2005, Sweatt had just arrived at the Indiana prison where he would spend the remainder of his life unless transferred. During our interview, he offered this apology statement while my partners and I listened. I wrote as he spoke. These are Sweatt's words as he said them:

> *"Regrettably sorry. Ask for forgiveness sincerely. Try to understand, just try to understand, even take time out, an hour out of your daily life. What would make a man come up with the idea to sit on people's porches as if he lived there? Not just Ms. Lou Edna Jones, even going in porches or backyards, stand in people's windows and look at an explosive device with you. If you can understand that, you know the person was crazy in that sense but not in another. He was able to live a secret life for so many years. To feel better about himself. It felt good setting fires. It was addictive to do it. It was exciting. Never thought of the consequences, because I didn't have a heart to hurt people, but I hurt for so many years. It became a happy feeling. I would rather hurt than to laugh or enjoy life. Now I have found peace, found rest. No more stress, no more people I can hurt. I have no right to have the freedom to do what I want. No right to terrorize the community. If I had one wish, it would be that I could be forgiven. If I can be forgiven, it will be over with. No one will talk to you about it. It will be behind me. I ask God for forgiveness nightly."*
>
> *"It will take a long time to get these horrible crimes out of my mind."*

FINAL THOUGHTS

The case involving Thomas Anthony Sweatt has been closed for fifteen years. Sweatt is in prison for the remainder of his natural life with no chance for parole. During his lifetime, he set hundreds—maybe even thousands—of fires causing thousands upon thousands of dollars in damage, and murdered four people. I say just four because nobody really knows how many people he may have killed. We were fortunate to have him admit to four. He had been setting fires from age fourteen until the time we arrested him at age fifty, so it is not unreasonable to assume that during all those years he may have killed additional people.

I'm not sure what people have in mind when they think about what a serial arsonist and murderer is supposed to look like, talk like, or even act like. For years, I locked up people who were setting fires, and today some fourteen years after retiring, I'm still not sure. I can tell you that most of those I dealt with when I locked them up had been in and out of trouble throughout their life, regardless of their age. Sweatt had minor scrapes with the law but was never really in trouble. Most arsonists I dealt with had issues with people of authority and some type of chip on their shoulders they simply could not shake off. For some, the chip was about race, some with their socioeconomic status, and yes, for some, it was because they were downright evil. I don't think Sweatt had issues with his race; he never expressed any to me. Sweatt loved people in uniform but had issues with authority. He wished for more status in life as most of us do. He was evil, but he kept that hidden well. Whenever I sat and talked with Sweatt—from the very first time we met in Southern Maryland—he was a gentleman, just another guy trying to make it like the rest of us.

He had a calm demeanor and appeared to be up on current events. He was neither vulgar nor angry. There were times it was really difficult to understand what he was saying. This wasn't because of some type of accent or because he was talking with slang. His voice was very soft and he just spoke quietly.

He was a nice guy. A hard working man having been with the same company for twenty years. He was well liked and the community where he lived and worked could not believe he was the serial arsonist after he was arrested. He did good work in the community, helped in the church, and worked hard keeping things looking nice in his neighborhood.

Nonetheless, what this man did not only affected the lives of all of his victims and their families, but also every single person who tracked and searched for him for twenty-two months. This guy came into my town, in the middle of my life, and into the lives of all the investigators, as well as our families. For two years, we placed a tremendous amount of our family time on hold trying to catch him, trying to stop the reign of terror he spread in the region. We were lucky and completed our case with an arrest and conviction. We got close to him, and even developed an understanding of him, or at least as much of an understanding as he wanted us to have.

I guess I still really don't know what a serial arsonist looks like. I was on the Task Force that chased the most dangerous and bizzare serial arsonist in American history. I was with him up close and personal, and even today I still wonder who the hell he is.

I came terrifyingly close to a tiger—and he rolled over and showed me his belly. When I think about Thomas Anthony Sweatt, I wonder what happened to him in his life to create a man that cast so much evil. A man that said he felt happiness when he was setting fires and never thought about those he was hurting in the process. No one can conclude for certain what took place in his childhood that made him this way. Maybe as one of the people who got the closest to hearing it from him, I should have some answers, but they would only be guesses—and that doesn't answer the question for me.

APPENDIX A

Case Facts

Every criminal investigation contains interesting facts unique to that case, and this one is no different. We might have had more media coverage than the average case because of the close proximity to the nation's capital, and we surely had access to many more resources than the average case because we have so many law enforcement agencies in the area, but a good portion of what made our case so interesting was innovative and hard working investigators using their knowledge and talent.

Scribing the bottoms of gallon jugs with a metal scribe to identify store locations and dates of purchase was simply genius. It was not some scientific step-by-step project pulled from a text book on investigation. It was the thought process of a local investigator sitting around a table with others trying to figure out a way to narrow the search area or to improve the means to catch the bad guy.

The "Black Bag Operation" was again not some scientific masterpiece; it was the work of several investigators talking about how they could develop a way to identify a store where some type of particular product was sold and when.

Attaching a numbered stainless steel chip the size of a dime inside a plastic bag and then placing that bag on a holder made up of a coffee can top, a hinge, and a metal rod was unreal. After seeing this project develop and then working with it for five months, I believe it should go into a textbook on investigations.

The development of an auto mugshot book was something I had always said would be useful. The Montgomery County police department had one and we used that as a template to establish ours. This book was nothing more than page after page after page of pictures of cars from different years, with different models and types. It is used no differently than when you provide a book of suspect pictures to a witness and ask them to go through it and identify someone that looks familiar. We had three witnesses that had seen our suspect for just a few minutes and, as part of that encounter, saw a vehicle. We worked the remainder of the case trying to identify that car. The development of the auto mugshot book made that job much easier.

Our case used every investigative tool available with the exception of a wiretap. We used a multitude of surveillance techniques that included video surveillance (both active and passive), human surveillance (active and static), air surveillance (infrared and heat detection surveillance). With the assistance of area agencies, after every fire we would dispatch an air unit to a particular community we were interested in. We would also send a car with two investigators. The air unit used infrared to determine which vehicles were still warm. The ground unit would write down the auto information and tag number and we would run the background on the owner. This process allowed us to develop a much longer list of suspects.

We used criminal search warrants and issued subpoenas for documents to summon people before the grand jury. We traced and tracked cell phone use and we used tracking devices on vehicles. We employed the use of K-9s in numerous ways. We used them to track scents and at the scene of fires to help determine the presence of accelerants.

We used hypnosis to gain information we had been unable to get any other way. We used Polaroid photography, aerial photography, 35mm photos, and digital photography.

We used the computer and the internet, tax records and wage earning slips. We used Division of Motor Vehicles records, we used social security files, and we used real property records and real estate files.

We talked with manufacturers and fabricators and dealt with store owners and heads of corporations. We did work with people in Europe and across the nation. We utilized federal laboratories, state laboratories, local laboratories, and private laboratories. We involved the local and national media in all forms: written, TV, radio and the web.

Simply stated, our investigative tools, techniques, equipment, and methods could teach both those new to investigations and seasoned members of the fire investigation and law enforcement communities how to work in a multi-agency Task Force.

The device used in setting the fires was unique. It was a modified "Molotov Cocktail." The device was placed, not thrown, and the wick was not placed inside the top of the container but wrapped around the handle. The components of the device were a one-gallon plastic jug filled with gasoline, and a cloth wick tied around or placed through the handle and concealed in a plastic bag.

DNA was found on different types of cloth material that had been exposed to various degrees of heat, and this case proved DNA can survive the heat of fire. The DNA found is what scientists call Low Copy, which means, simply, anyone who touches something leaves a certain amount of his or her DNA on the object touched. Low Copy DNA is a profiling technique developed by the UK and has been in use there since 1999. This was the first case I was aware of in the US that used the technique.

We ran the DNA profile we had in The Combined DNA Index System (CODIS), which is the National Database created and maintained by the FBI on a monthly basis with no hits. We also ran it in the Maryland and Virginia DNA databases monthly, and again never got a hit.

We had three eyewitnesses that saw the arsonist. We used a computer-based program to create a drawing and we had brought in a sketch artist to create a drawing. In both instances the final image came from the information these witnesses provided. After Sweatt was arrested, his picture was shown to them and interestingly enough, none of the three confirmed that the picture was of the same man that had approached their car. Eyewitness testimony can only be a tool.

The Task Force handled 2950 leads, interviewed 1368 people as possible suspects, handled 279 separate events, visited 688 separate fire locations, photographed and reviewed over 350 vehicles, and processed over 200 pieces of property. At the height of the case, there were 65 investigators assigned from 35 different local, state, and federal agencies. Our investigators wrote over 3120 narratives in the 22-month investigation.

Several times during the course of the investigation, I tried to make sense of what was going on. I felt there had to be some link we were missing. I conducted searches of street names and then tried to develop a process based on the number of letters, the month, the day of the week, or anything that I thought would fit. DC had the most fires, then Prince George's County, and finally Virginia. I made a chart dealing with three garden apartment fires we had at the time and studied that trying to learn the arsonist's pattern for selecting his target.

As the chart shows, there was no real pattern, yet it showed the arsonist liked certain things.

Case coincidences included: two different occasions the Task Force made internal announcements on changes to take place and each time a fire took place. There were fires in December 2003 and January 2004 that took place within two miles of the Task Force operations center, one to the north and one to the south. There were two times when two fires took place on the same night: Thursday, June 5, 2004, and Tuesday, June 17, 2004.

On February 4, 2004, a fire took place in the middle of the day at 1456 hours. This was also a day the Task Force commanders made a presentation to all the area police and fire agencies at the ATF lab. This fire also marked a change in how the arsonist was placing the device. The placement was lying on its side instead of upright. The

55th Ave. PG County, MD	7101 Richmond Hwy. Fairfax, VA	7700 Blair Rd. Montgomery County, MD
0311	1500	0456
Brick Exterior	Brick Exterior	Brick Exterior
Metal Stairs	Metal Stairs	Concrete & Metal Stairs
Masonry Walls	Masonry Walls	Sheet rock walls
1st Floor Stairs	Ground floor in front of door	Landing between 1&2
1 gal. jug	1 gal. jug	1 gal. jug
sitting straight up	laying sideways	laying sideways
black bag	black bag	black & white bag
black cloth wick	black cloth wick	black cloth wick
unknown type of jug	classic spring water	classic spring water
1 caller	unknown on callers	multi callers
no injuries	no injuries	3 injuries
4-story building	4-story building	4-story building
no security	no security	no security
woodline path in rear	woodline in front	park area in front
open entry	open entry	open entry
front & rear exits	front & rear exits	front & rear exits
no cameras	no cameras	no cameras
gasoline	gasoline	gasoline

fire on January 22, 2004, which took place on 55th Avenue in PG County marked a change in building type. The arsonist moved from single-family homes to garden apartments. Twice the arsonist took long breaks, one lasting sixty-two days and one lasting sixty-four days. On both occasions, when the arsonist re-started setting fires, he went to the same neighborhood in PG County known as Birchwood City. One took place on Thursday and one on Friday.

There was only one fire in the City of Alexandria and it was the only location that was not in a primarily working class neighborhood. This fire took place five days after a fire on 24th Street in DC where it is believed Task Force members were seen by the arsonist as they arrived almost as soon as the fire companies. There were no additional fires in DC for eight months after this.

After the townhouse fire in the Rosecroft Village community in PG county, the victim received a threat letter in the mail one week later. This was the fire where the mother of the victim called the arsonist names on TV.

There was only one fire where we found two devices. This fire took place on a Friday in PG County.

APPENDIX B
Additional Case Photos

Suspect drawing by Lois Gibson
Image from author's files

CRITICAL WITNESS

B/M 5'9" TALL, MED BUILD, DARK COMPLECTED
Last seen wearing a dark blue baseball cap, burgundy colored
t-shirt and dark colored pants.

The Metropolitan Police Department is currently investigating a suspicious fire that occurred in the 2500 block
of Randolph Rd., N.E. on Monday, June 30, 2003, at approximately 4:00 in the morning. The witness
(depicted above) was last seen riding a dark colored "mountain" bicycle headed toward Eastern Ave., N.E.
Anyone with information about this crime or the identity of this witness is asked to call:

MPDC SOC HOTLINE:

Drawing of witness who saw suspect at fire in DC in June 2003
Image from author's files

Letter from Sweatt to Fulkerson in September 2005 (page 1)
Image from author's files

Letter from Sweatt to Fulkerson in September 2005 (page 2)
Image from author's files

COMMON TRAITS

1. All fires have been intentionally set.
2. All are set to the exterior of occupied single-family homes.
3. All fires are in the early hours (0200 to 0600 hours).
4. All fires involve an ignitable liquid.
5. All fires involve a plastic jug.

THINGS TO LOOK FOR

1. Anyone carrying a jug or heavy bag.
2. Anyone seen hanging around parks, a wood line, or playground.
3. Anyone carrying gas cans or jugs in their vehicle.
4. Anyone parked in a vehicle for an extended period of time in an area of single-family homes.

ACTIONS

1. Please complete a field observation report and obtain an accurate address.
2. Any vehicle stops; obtain name, and vehicle description.
3. Anyone you encounter that you feel fits the above and you believe the task force should talk to, call (301) 583-1878. If no answer, contact communications and ask for a Prince George's County Fire Investigator.
4. Take a picture whenever possible. (Digital if available)
5. Place "Copy to Arson Task Force" on the top of the field observation report, and turn the report in.

Law Enforcement Use Only!

Do NOT Disseminate!

PRINCE GEORGE'S COUNTY FIRE/EMS DEPARTMENT • DISTRICT OF COLUMBIA FIRE AND EMS DEPARTMENT • BUREAU OF ALCOHOL, TOBACCO, FIREARMS, & EXPLOSIVES • PRINCE GEORGE'S COUNTY POLICE DEPARTMENT • METROPOLITAN POLICE DEPARTMENT • OFFICE OF THE STATE FIRE MARSHAL • MARYLAND • ANNE ARUNDEL COUNTY FIRE DEPARTMENT • MONTGOMERY COUNTY DEPARTMENT OF FIRE & RESCUE SERVICES • MARYLAND STATE POLICE • PRINCE GEORGE'S COUNTY OFFICE OF THE SHERIFF • ALEXANDRIA FIRE DEPARTMENT • HOWARD COUNTY DEPARTMENT OF FIRE/RESCUE SERVICES • HOWARD COUNTY POLICE DEPARTMENT

Flyer used when briefing law enforcement agencies
Image from author's files

MD – DC – VA – ATF
ARSON TASK FORCE

```
                    ┌──────────────┐
                    │  Case Agent  │
                    └──────────────┘
        ┌─────────────────┐   ┌─────────────────┐
        │      Asst       │   │   Case Agent    │
        │   Case Agent    │   │   Records Mgt   │
        └─────────────────┘   └─────────────────┘
        ┌─────────────────┐   ┌─────────────────┐
        │  Investigations │   │ Evidence Section│
        │    Supervisor   │   │    Supervisor   │
        └─────────────────┘   └─────────────────┘
        ┌─────────────────┐   ┌─────────────────┐
        │  General Leads  │   │ Physical Evidence│
        └─────────────────┘   └─────────────────┘
        ┌─────────────────┐   ┌─────────────────┐
        │  Tip Line Leads │   │    Supplies     │
        └─────────────────┘   └─────────────────┘
        ┌─────────────────┐   ┌─────────────────┐
        │   Scene Canvas  │   │ Case Data Bases │
        └─────────────────┘   └─────────────────┘
        ┌─────────────────┐   ┌─────────────────┐
        │   Sueveillance  │   │  Administration │
        │                 │   │      leave      │
        │                 │   │    schedules    │
        └─────────────────┘   └─────────────────┘
        ┌─────────────────┐   ┌─────────────────┐
        │Suspect Development│ │  Case Analysis  │
        └─────────────────┘   └─────────────────┘
        ┌─────────────────┐   ┌─────────────────┐
        │     Victims     │   │  Agency Liaison │
        └─────────────────┘   └─────────────────┘
```

PRINCE GEORGE'S COUNTY FIRE/EMS • DEPARTMENT DISTRICT OF COLUMBIA FIRE/EMS • DEPARTMENT BUREAU OF ALCOHOL, TOBACCO, FIREARMS, & EXPLOSIVES • PRINCE GEORGE'S COUNTY POLICE DEPARTMENT• METROPOLITAN POLICE DEPARTMENT•

Task Force Organizational Structure
Image from author's files

ROBERT M. LUCKETT

Task Force Statement

"The Task Force would like the person responsible for these fires to contact us, either through our phone tip line, our post office box, or email address. From our understanding of individuals involved in this type of behavior, we know they often desire to communicate a message to society at large. We want this person to know that we are a willing audience for that message. We hope he may be watching, or listening to this request. We feel we may understand him and can relate to him.

This firesetting may be a means for him to relieve stress or frustration caused by other people. This stress may be borne out of some type of anger or unwanted feeling of powerlessness. In a complex world, especially at this time, we can all understand what stress is. This individual may feel pain and anger more than the average person and therefore chose to relieve those feelings through firesetting. We understand.

It may be that this firesetting, which at first may have made him feel powerful, has become like a drug, the use of which may be getting out of control. That is understandable. This person may not have had the best of home lives growing up and is suffering now as an adult for it. He may himself have been victimized in his past. One way he can truly relieve his pain and regain control is to seek assistance with the pain and anger he is feeling. It may also be that this firesetting, even though it may cause him anxiety, may also have an exciting, if not thrilling, aspect to it. Again, we understand this and will not hold those feelings against him.

From our experience with these types of cases, we know that it is most probable that we will identify and apprehend this person. If he does choose to contact us first and help us understand him, it will go a long way in how he is dealt with by authorities. He may not realize how much he has the power to control his destiny and one first step in doing that is to contact people who understand him. We are also concerned that innocent people will continue to be in harm's way as a result of this firesetting. This concern extends to him as well. Accidents can happen to the best of us and we do not want to see him get hurt either.

So on behalf of the Task Force and the entire Fire Service community at large, we request that the person involved in these incidents contact us at the numbers or addresses listed below."

301-77-ARSON (301-772-7766)

PRINCE GEORGE'S COUNTY FIRE/EMS DEPARTMENT • DISTRICT OF COLUMBIA FIRE AND EMS

Plea to the arsonist in September 2003
Image from author's files

ARSON REWARD $35,000

The **DC · ATF · MD · VA Arson Task Force** is offering **$35,000** for information leading to the arrest and conviction of the person(s) responsible for a series of fires in the Prince George's County, DC and Virginia area.

Believed to be linked by the Arson Task Force:

June 13, 2003 - 3800 Ellis Street., Capital Heights, MD
June 17, 2003 - 5800 Jefferson Heights Drive, Capital Heights, MD
June 20, 2003 - 1300 Chapel Oaks Drive, Capital Heights, MD
June 21, 2003 - 2400 Wintergreen Avenue, District Heights, MD
June 22, 2003 - 1500 Ruston Avenue, Capital Heights, MD
June 25, 2003 - 4900 North Capital Street, NW., Washington, DC
September 4, 2003 - 5100 block of Barnaby Run Drive, Oxon Hill, MD
September 8, 2003 - 200 Quackenbos Street. NW., Washington, DC
September 10, 2003 - 4700 block of Dix Street, NE., Washington, DC
September 14, 2003 - 4100 block of Anacostia Avenue, NE., Washington, DC
October 8, 2003 - 1300 Otis St., NE., Washington, DC
November 11, 2003 - 1700 block of 24th Street, Washington, DC
November 16, 2003 - 4400 block of West Braddock Road, Alexandria, VA
December 20, 2003 - 5700 block of 83rd Place, New Carrollton, MD
January 22, 2004 - 3400 block of 55th Avenue, Bladensburg, MD

All of these fires or attempted fires have occurred during early morning hours

If you have any information regarding these crimes, please call the
ARSON TASK FORCE at **301-77-ARSON** or **301-772-7766**.

Prince George's Co. Fire/EMS Department · District of Columbia Fire/EMS Department · Bureau of Alcohol, Tobacco, Firearms & Explosives · Prince George's Co. Police Department · Metropolitan Police Department · Office of the State Fire Marshal · Anne Arundel Co Fire Department · Montgomery Co. Department of Fire & Rescue · Maryland State Police · Prince George's Co. Office of the Sheriff · Alexandria Fire Department · Howard Co. Department of Fire/Rescue Services · Howard Co. Police Department

Task Force Arson Reward Poster
Image from author's files

ROBERT M. LUCKETT

U.S. Department of Justice

United States Attorney
District of Maryland
Northern Division

Rod J. Rosenstein
United States Attorney

Vickie E. LeDuc
Public Information Officer

36 South Charles Street
Fourth Floor
Baltimore, Maryland 21201

410-209-4800
TTY/TDD:410-962-4462
410-209-4885
FAX 410-962-3091
Vickie.LeDuc@usdoj.gov

SEPTEMBER 12, 2005
FOR IMMEDIATE RELEASE
www.usdoj.gov/usao/md

FOR FURTHER
INFORMATION CONTACT
VICKIE E. LEDUC
410-209-4885

"SERIAL ARSONIST" THOMAS SWEATT SENTENCED TO LIFE IN PRISON FOR SETTING 45 RESIDENTIAL FIRES IN MARYLAND, DISTRICT OF COLUMBIA AND VIRGINIA

Fires Resulted in Two Deaths

GREENBELT, Maryland - United States Attorneys for the District of Maryland Rod J. Rosenstein, for the District of Columbia Kenneth L. Wainstein, and for the Eastern District of Virginia Paul J. McNulty, and Bureau of Alcohol, Tobacco, Firearms and Explosives Special Agent in Charge Theresa R. Stoop announce that today U.S. District Court Judge Deborah K. Chasanow sentenced Thomas Sweatt, age 51, of Washington, D.C., to life in prison in connection with his guilty plea to possession of destructive devices; destruction of buildings by fire resulting in personal injury; possession of destructive devices in furtherance of a crime of violence; first degree premeditated murder (felony murder) and second degree murder.

Maryland United States Attorney Rod J. Rosenstein stated, "I am profoundly grateful to the skilled investigators, prosecutors and scientists who worked tirelessly to catch Mr. Sweatt and bring his senseless crime wave to an end. More fires would have been set, more homes would have been destroyed, and more people would have been killed if not for the extraordinary work of federal, state and local law enforcement agencies and the assistance of private citizens and businesses."

United States Attorney Kenneth Wainstein stated "Over the course of two years, Mr. Sweatt methodically terrorized people in every corner of the Washington Metropolitan Region. At the same time, the dedicated public servants on the Serial Arson Task Force just as methodically tracked him down and built a solid case that led to his conviction and life sentence. It is our hope that today's sentence will provide a measure of comfort and justice for our many neighbors who suffered at the hands of Mr. Sweatt."

ATF Special Agent in Charge Theresa Stoop stated "For over two years each member of the

United States Department of Justice memo
on sentencing of Thomas Anthony Sweatt
Image from author's files

229

task force worked feverishly for this day. Although we cannot resurrect the precious lives of Lou Edna Jones or Annie Brown, repair the destroyed property, or erase the horrible memories caused by Mr. Sweatt's crimes, we hope this life sentence will foster healing for all in our communities."

According to the agreed statement of facts presented to the court as part of his plea agreement, Sweatt deliberately set a series of fires in Maryland, the District of Columbia and Virginia in 2003 and 2004, understanding that his actions would result in damage and injury to persons and property. Sweatt set 45 residential fires using incendiary devices, the components of which were a one-gallon plastic jug, a plastic bag, and a cloth material used as a wick. Gasoline was used as an accelerant in the devices.

According to the statement of facts, investigators from the Serial Arson Task Force were able to identify Sweatt as the perpetrator of the arsons by, among other things, matching DNA samples recovered at various fire scenes. Upon his arrest on April 27, 2005, Sweatt admitted in a videotaped confession to Task Force Agents that he typically placed the device near a door because it was more likely to burn at that location and that he was, at times, aware that persons were in the homes at which he set these devices on fire.

For example, an investigation of a fire on February 5, 2002 at 1210 Montello Avenue, N.E., Washington, D.C. revealed that smoke from the fire seeped through the walls to the adjoining house where 89-year-old Annie Brown resided. Ms. Brown suffered from smoke inhalation and was taken to the hospital where she died on February 14, 2002.

Also, on June 5, 2003 firefighters were called to 2800 Evarts Street, N.E, Washington, D.C. where they found the house totally engulfed in flames. Two occupants had escaped by jumping from a second-story window. Firefighters rescued 86-year-old Lou Edna Jones from her second-floor bedroom where she had been trapped. She was taken to Washington Hospital Center where she was pronounced dead. A subsequent investigation revealed that the fire was intentionally set by a device containing an ignitable liquid which was placed outside near the front door. The fire penetrated the interior first floor and made its way up the stairwell to the second floor.

Additionally, a device containing ignitable liquid was placed between the first and second floors of an apartment building's only stairwell at 7700 Blair Road, Silver Spring, Maryland. An investigation of this February 14, 2004 fire revealed that the burning ignitable liquid flowed across the landing and down the steps to the first floor. The fire produced untenable heat, smoke and combustion, forcing the occupants to jump from second and third story windows, resulting in physical injuries.

Sweatt admitted setting each of these and other fires, and pleaded guilty to charges of murder.

United States Attorney Rosenstein commended the outstanding investigative work performed over the past two years by the Serial Arson Task Force, which includes the Bureau of Alcohol, Tobacco, Firearms and Explosives; District of Columbia Fire/EMS; Prince George's County Fire/EMS Department; District of Columbia Metropolitan Police Department; Prince George's County Police; Maryland State Fire Marshals Office ; Montgomery County Department of Fire and

Rescue Services; Montgomery County Police Department; Fairfax County Fire and Rescue; Maryland State Police; Anne Arundel County Fire; Alexandria Fire Department; Howard County Fire Department; Howard County Police Department; Arlington County Fire Department; and Baltimore City Fire Department. Mr. Rosenstein also thanked the Naval Criminal Investigative Service for their valuable assistance.

Mr. Rosenstein also praised Assistant U.S. Attorneys Mythili Raman and James M. Trusty from the District of Maryland, Jennifer Anderson from the District of Columbia and Morris Parker from the Eastern District of Virginia, who prosecuted the case.

United States Department of Justice memo
on sentencing of Thomas Anthony Sweatt
Image from author's files

ROBERT M. LUCKETT

1. 3300 7th Street S.E. (Montaray Park) - residential under construction – device – 330 to 430 am time frame – year 2003
2. 3324 Wheeler Road S.E. –marked police car – device under L front tire – 5 am – year 2003
3. 4320 Livingston Rd. S.E. – Black Yukon – device placed on top of tire – early am around 4 – year 2004
4. 3800 Zenixa intersection with 2 nd St. –Yukon – device under L front tire – 330 to 430 am – year 2003
5. 3988 2nd St. S.W. – rear of home by door – device – early am – year 2002
6. 3840 South Capital St. – inside hall by rear apt door - 2nd floor- device – Noon to 1 pm – year 2001
7. 3027 MLK – rear of bldg – walk up stairs – device – 2 to 3 am – year 1999 to 2000 – (this location was residential, torn down and now commercial)
8. 546 Labaum – basement in the rear – device – 630 am – year 1999
9. 552 Labaum – basement in the rear – device – 430 am – year 1999
10. 2392 Iverson St – Temple Hills Md. – Hillcrest Carry Out – rear window- Pour – ignited a heater – 230 to 330 am – year 2001
11. 460 Labaum – rear porch – device – early am – year 1998 or 1999
12. Milwaukee Place – Boys and Girls Club – down steps – entrance door to gym- device – early am – year 1995
13. 245 Newcomb St – Blue Yukon – device R front tire – early am – year 2004
14. 254 2nd St. – Blazer – device – L front tire – early am – year 1998 to 1999
15. 400 Orange St – Blue, Yukon – device – early am – R front tire – year 2004 followed man from liquor, set the device- drove away-returned and set fire
16. Malcolm X & 2nd Street – Car – device – R rear – 130 to 2 am – year 2004
17. 3423 5th Street – East Gate Condos – gray car – device – front of car- early am year 2002
18. 3425 5th Street – East Gate Condos – unk SUV – device – front of vehicle – early am – year 2002
19. 1810 or 1812 Alabama Ave. S.E. – residential under construction – device set in basement- walker up from rear – early am – year 2003- 1 firefighter injury – fell through floor into basement – paper accounts blamed poor construction. Burned along time.
20. 1223 Good Hope Road – side of bldg. – Pour – early am 330 to 430 am –year 2001
21. 1907 Good Hope Road – Kings Court Condos – silver gray car – device – L front tire – early am - year 2003 to 2004
22. 2412 Pomeroy St. – Black Ford- Pick- Up Truck – device – L front tire – early am – year 2003 – Note : this fire ignited 4 other cars

Notes from the Task Force Ridealongs with Thomas Anthony Sweatt
Page 1
Image from the author's files

23. 2315 Evans St. – S.E. – gray car – device – front vehicle by motor – early am – device – year 2001 – Note : this fire extended to the car port.

24. 2607 Bowen – Oxford Manor Apts – truck – hot rod – early am – device – R front of vehicle – year 2004

25. 1300 blk of O St –(intersection of) O and Half St – Metro Bus Yard – device – daytime, 2 pm – Black Mercedes – rear of car – winter time – year 2003 – Note: this fire extended to a second car.

26. 1200 Blk of Half St – Corner of M and Half – Metro employee parking lot – Red Durango- device – R front tire – early am – year 2004

27. 801 I Street – auto unk type – marine sticker on window – device – daytime about 4 pm - year 2003

28. 657 I Street – Black Navigator – device – L front tire – early am – year 2004

29. 4815 B – Annapolis Rd 0 Bladensberg Shopping Center – Cleaners – rear of location set in the window – device – early am – 2001 to 2002

30. 1717 Hamlin (across from) – marked police car – device – R front tire – 130 to 330 am – year 2002

31. 200 P Street N.W. – apt bldg – set fire in hallway lower level by door-Big pair of work boots by door – apt was on right – Pour – gasoline – early am 1 to 2 am – year 1984 to 1986 – Was driving sisters car, a burgundy camero - left scene came back, parked and went into crowd to watch. Hear people talking about how victims looked. Saw one man brought out on stretcher. DOA – knees bent in his underwear. Baby burned – think it lived –Another person injured. Fire was in the winter

32. 61, 63, 65 or 67 Quincy Place N.W. – Row House – Pour – used a long towel by door on front porch – early am – year 1984 to 1986 – Saw man walking from bus stop. Parked his car – burgundy camero on First Street, got out his car and walked toward man. Saw him enter house and set fire on the porch – Drove past several times saw them jumping out windows – man in basement calling for help – rear newspaper accounts. When fire trucks arrived went home- Believe mans name was ROY PEACOCK- mans wife also died. Fire was in the winter. Mr. Sweat indicated that his attorney had his investigator look into this and he found no records of a Mr. Peacocks death.

33. 1215 3rd Street – N.E. –unmarked police car – device – rear – early am –year 2003

34. 1215 3rd Street N. E. – marked police car – device – rear – early am – 2003

35. Rear of United Auto Sales on 3rd Street N.E. – car unk type – device – rear of car – year 2003. Fire extended to 2 other cars

36. 126 34 Street N.E. – apt bldg – hallway straight in near laundry room – right side apt door – device – placed near trash can – reports that the trash can was set on fire – 3 to 4 am – year 2001 to 2002. Drove past several times – screams for help. Read about 1 Injury.

37. 2 or 4 Ridge Road S. E. – home sunder construction – set in rear – device – 330 to 430 time frame – total burn down – year 2003

Notes from the Task Force Ridealongs with Thomas Anthony Sweatt
Page 2
Image from the author's files

Totals	Residential -	Commercial -	Vehicles
44	14	3	27

1 – Firefighter Injury at 1810 to 1812 Alabama Avenue – 2003

1 DOA – 200 P Street N.W.–1984 to 1986
2 Injuries – 200 P Street N.W. – 1984 to 1986 1 injury was a baby

2 DOA's – 61 to 67 Quincy Place N.W. – man and wife – man's name is believed to Roy Peacock –

1 Injury – 126 34th Street S.E. – 2001 to 2002

Robert M. Luckett   Date
Chief Deputy Fire Marshal
Alexandria Fire Department

Notes from the Task Force Ridealongs with Thomas Anthony Sweatt
Page 3
Image from the author's files

APPENDIX C
Lessons Learned

This section is intended for investigator education.

While I do not know of any place to find all the answers to all the things one will come across during an investigation, it is nice to to fall back on those who have experienced it before. This is just a small list of things that can and should be reviewed along the way in your investigations. Remember, if small investigations are conducted the same way as your large ones it will be easy when the big one strikes. Allow me to offer an example. When investigating a suspicious room and contents fire, you must conduct witness interviews, owners, 911 caller, and first arriving fire crews. Document the scene with drawings and photographs. Locate, examine, package, and collect evidence. These items are generally done in a timely fashion. The same is true for larger incidents. The major difference is the number of people assigned to the job and the number of people to interview is greater. Investigators have to be conscientious and consistent. Ask questions if you don't know; somebody does. Take the time to get the appropriate number of people and resources available to do the job. Don't rush, take your time, and follow all the steps you know that need to be done.

Common Communication Systems Between Agencies

You must have a system available that allows people from multiple agencies to communicate. Portable radios are a consideration because of the two-way communication, but generally will not have the ability to receive all jurisdictions involved. You may find they are also isolated to just either fire or police. With today's technology I would look at using smartphones and look at all the apps available that might work if they would be secure.

Communication Devices

Nextel phones were what we used. They provided two-way communication, crossed both the fire and police boundaries, and provided the investigators with a phone at all times. Today we have smartphones and just about everyone in the world has one.

Agency Commitment

There must be a FULL COMMITMENT from the chief and the political powers from the beginning. Once committed to being a part of a Task Force, your commitment has to be until the end, no matter how long it takes. When an investigator is assigned to the case, it has to be someone the agency is willing to allow to be part of the investigation until the end. This is a must. The agency cannot require the assigned investigator to carry a heavy workload in his or her office and the workload of the Task Force.

Agencies often want to be a part when there is a good deal of action or media coverage, but when things slow down they want to bow out. As long as the Task Force is active, you must remain involved. Administrators must be fully versed in what a commitment to the Task Force may mean in terms of time away from normal duties and the potential costs. Federal involvement is a fiscal godsend. The use of inter-local agreements prior to an incident like this can relieve some of the strain and secure cooperation, resource sharing, and predesignated staffing allowances. Political interference must be avoided.

Establish Infrastructure Early

The establishment of infrastructure at an early stage in an investigation is critical. The framework has to be one that everyone can work in. You will be mixing multiple agencies and multiple approaches. Develop how your unit is going to work and then put all of the people involved in a room and explain the entire process. Whatever your process is going to be, put it on paper. When a new player comes on board they are able to review your basic operational plan and know ahead of time if they can commit to being a part of the team. Develop a Memorandum of Understanding (MOU) for each agency and investigator to read and sign before they join. Be sure to cover commitment, overtime costs, work hours, response, chain of command, media relations, and confidentiality. This is critical to the success or lack of success in large scale multi-jurisdictional incidents.

Information Management

Information management could be the single most important decision during an investigation. You must have a single system that can be accessed remotely by all the agencies involved. The system should be stand-alone, and should be able to operate independent from any other system which might be brought in. It should have the capability to add new users as the case moves along. You should also limit the number of people who add data to the system to ensure consistency. The system should be read-only.

Prioritizing Leads

You must have a process to prioritize. You will have leads that come in that may sound so far fetched that your investigators feel they are wasting their time. All leads have to be followed-up, but you should categorize them as high, medium, and low. Everyone involved should have the chance to work the high or hot leads as well as the low priority leads. It is easy to forget about leads and the person supervising this section needs to have a system for tracking them and making sure they are completed. A successful investigation depends on proper assessment and assignment of ALL leads.

Tip Line

A formal process must be established early. How will your phone lines be answered, whether via tape or live person? How will the call be processed? What information will the call-taker be required to get? Who pays for the line? When you do a press release or make a plea to the public, you must have extra staff to handle the calls.

Information Leaks

When there is a high-profile case that affects an entire town, city, or region, everyone wants to impress others with how much they know about it. You must take steps to reduce the amount of information being placed in people's hands to prevent the media from trying to run your case. Leaks go directly to the media. Information leaks will be part of every investigation but cannot be the focus of the investigation. This sometimes happens. Consider having every investigator assigned to the unit sign an integrity agreement. They also need to know that if they are found to be releasing information improperly they will be excused from the operation and could face charges. In today's world you have an added feature that will have to be addressed on a regular basis: social media. I suggest you establish an internal policy on how to handle your social media issues and have every investigator agree to it up front. If you don't address, this your case will be on the different social media forums way more than you can handle. Information sharing should include your PIOs and others that may interact with the media. The primary spokesperson does not need to know every detail or potential sensitive issues. It's important for this person to be able to say, "I don't know."

Media Relations

Reporters can be your best friends or your worst friends. You need to understand that at some point in your investigation you will need them. It is a very fine line working with reporters, but you must do it.

Establish a single spokesperson for the Task Force, assigned the duty for the duration. Have regular press briefings and press conferences. Try to establish a single location to conduct the process each time. Lucky for us we had the fire chief from PG County Fire and Rescue as our spokesperson. Chief Blackwell could not have handled all the political and departmental issues that surrounded him any better than he did and we were far better off with him than people from the other agencies, mine included. The man was pulled in so many directions, I thought he was going to turn into taffy. Provide the media with printed material they can use to help you. They can distribute more information than you can and in a much faster way.

Be sure to keep all the public information officers from every agency informed, but also make sure that they have a reduced role. Remember you must have a single spokesperson.

Evidence Procedures

There must be a single process for collecting your evidence and there needs to be one group of people collecting it each and every time. All the evidence collected needs to go to the same lab every time you collect something. Investigators must package and label the evidence the same each and every time. There must be an open and positive communication process with your lab. The evidence group should meet and discuss what is going on with the lab on a regular basis.

Establish a Scene Investigation Protocol

Having scene management is important and having each and every investigator work in the same consistent manner is important. Your scene process should be on paper to allow any new person coming in to know what is expected of them and what needs to be done. Consider the development of a scene investigation kit. Place all forms in the kit along with canvass sheets, blank recording media, interview sheets, sketch paper, etc.

Direct Access to MVA/DMV

You need a driver's license picture daily, and without having direct access to these agencies, it will slow your investigation process.

Common Law Enforcement Procedures

You cannot take for granted that everyone knows how to do something just because they are a law enforcement officer. Plan your procedures and conduct preoperative briefings to outline everyone's duties and responsibilities. Cover your use-of-force policy, determine routes of travel, routes of escape, and all the basic law enforcement elements.

In-house Training

Provide training to your investigators on topics that will help your case like special techniques of interviewing, dealing with the public, and other classes that will help.

Common Task Force Credentials

Every person involved in the investigation needs to have the same credentials. Your efforts need to be unified. There needs to be a single ID card for everyone and a single business card for everyone.

Morale

To keep your operation moving forward and keep everyone focused, you need to stay in touch with the morale of your staff. Task Force operations demand very long hours and often produce very small results. Take time to make sure your people are okay.

Encourage them to seek help if they need it, keep an open line of communication with their families, and do things as a group. Sounds corny, but bonding is important. Morale goes up and down.

SOLVING FOR X

ARSON TASK FORCE

MD/DC/VA
ARSON TASK FORCE

CONFIDENTIAL TIP LINE 301-772.7766
DIRECT LINE 301-345-9253

email: 77ARSON@co.pg.md.us

ROBERT LUCKETT

CHIEF DEPUTY FIRE
MARSHAL
CITY OF ALEXANDRIA

STATE OF MARYLAND
OFFICE OF THE
STATE FIRE MARSHAL

THIS CERTIFIES THAT:

ROBERT LUCKETT

P. G. DIST. OF COLUMBIA ARSON TASK FORCE
INVESTIGATOR

HAS BEEN APPOINTED SPECIAL ASSISTANT STATE FIRE
MARSHAL FOR THE YEAR 2004

Task force credentials used by the author during the case
(Images courtesy of the author's files)

Investigator Input

Do nothing that will inhibit your investigators from speaking their mind. They need to have buy-in at all times. During your briefing sessions, encourage them to offer ideas for the investigation. It is also important to keep them on point and do not allow them to offer investigative ideas that have no foundation.

Seek Advice from Experience

Consider talking with people who have handled the same types of investigation. Allow them to review what you are doing and make suggestions for improvement.

Bring them to your operation if possible and take them to some of your scenes. Fresh ideas from someone who has been there is invaluable.

War Room

Consider the creation of a location that has all your case information laid out for all investigators to see at a glance. There are volumes of information gathered each day and no one can be expected to recall everything. Having a location where they can go and look at something is a tremendous help. Allow your imagination to work. The more information you can make available the better.

We created a place where anyone could go and look at the information we had on hand. It was based on the same approach the lab had set up for us with evidence. Every single fire had its own information board. The board contained everything we knew about that incident. A picture of the location, tax records, owners names, people interviewed, vehicles looked at, day of the week, time, construction type. When you looked at the boards you could see at a glance how many times a person's name came up and how many incidents they were tied to, how many cars were seen at the same incident, etc. This room, along with our case books, provided invaluable information.

Case Files or Case Books

Consider making a separate file or book on each incident. Every piece of information relating to that incident goes into the file or book. Select investigators in the group to be subject-matter experts on each file or book and make them responsible for keeping the information updated and current. This allows you to go to a single place and access the information, and it is portable as well.

Trust

This will be one of the hardest things to achieve and one of the easiest things to lose. Everyone in the investigation must check their egos at the door.

You cannot talk about the need for trusting other agencies and not be willing to give it yourself.

Know Your Players

Plan now for the future. Get to know the people in all the agencies around your area: state, federal, and local. Establish regular meetings and share common information. Establish regular training programs and have people from all the different agencies involved.

ACKNOWLEDGMENTS

I have never written a book of any type and until I started this, I would never even consider writing one. After the case was over and after talking with many of the people involved, I felt a need to write. What is written here is simply my view of the facts of what happened along a two-year journey. I feel there is much to be learned from our case, both the successes and failures, and hope perhaps this serves as a teaching tool for future investigators. Thomas Anthony Sweatt is the most dangerous and bizarre arsonist of all time, and what he provided to us is a unique story that everyone needs to know. I hope you find reading the story as interesting as I found being a part of it.

While I cannot use the names of all the men and women who were a part of the case, I want thank each one of them for making my life richer by having had the chance to meet and get to know them. All the experiences I shared, even with those whom I had bad experiences, was great and I would not have changed it for a second.

The following agencies assisted in our investigation in some fashion:

- Alexandria Virginia Fire Marshal's Office
- Alexandria Virginia Fire Department
- Alexandria Virginia Police Department
- Arlington Virginia Fire Marshal's Office
- Arlington Virginia Police Department
- Fairfax Virginia Fire Marshal's Office
- Fairfax Virginia Police Department

- Prince William County Virginia Fire Marshal's Office
- City of Manassas Virginia Fire Marshal's Office
- District of Colombia Fire Department
- Metropolitan Washington Police Department
- United States Park Police
- Prince George's County Maryland Fire Department
- Prince George's County Maryland Police Department
- Metropolitan Police Intelligence
- Maryland State Police
- Maryland State Fire Marshal's Office
- Montgomery County Maryland Police Crime Lab
- Montgomery County Maryland Police Department
- Montgomery County Maryland. Fire Marshal's Office
- Baltimore City Maryland Fire Marshal's Office
- ATF Kansas City Office
- ATF Falls Church Virginia Office
- ATF Baltimore Field Office
- ATF Hyattsville Maryland Office
- ATF Philadelphia Office
- Federal Bureau of Investigation (Quantico)
- Anne Arundel County Maryland Fire Marshal's Office
- ATF Atlanta Office
- ATF Kentucky Office ATF New York Office
- ATF Chicago Office ATF Ohio Office
- Howard County Maryland Fire Marshal's Office
- Howard County Maryland Police Department

- ATF Raleigh North Carolina Office
- ATF Wilmington North Carolina Office
- Loudoun County Virginia Fire Marshal's Office
- US Customs Service
- Maryland Division of Motor Vehicles
- Virginia Division of Motor Vehicles
- DC Division of Motor Vehicles
- Metropolitan Washington Police Department
- Metropolitan Police Washington Police Intelligence
- US Marshals Service
- ATF Tennessee Office
- ATF Detroit Office
- ATF Rochester New York Office
- ATF Norfolk Virginia Office
- ATF West Virginia Office
- ATF Washington Field Office
- Anne Arundel County Maryland Police Department
- ATF Baltimore Maryland Field Office
- ATF Delaware Office
- ATF National Lab

REFERENCES &

WORKS CITED

Abrahamsen, David. *Confessions of Son of Sam*. New York, Columbia University Press, 1985.

Antholis, Kary. "A Convicted Fireman-Arsonist and Me: The Beginning." *Crime Story*, 3 Dec. 2019, crimestory.com/2019/12/03/a-convicted-fireman-arsonist-and-me-the-beginning/. Accessed 24 Jan. 2020.

Associated Press. "Maryland Housing Arson Probed as Hate Crime." 16 Dec. 2004, www.nbcnews.com/id/wbna6725478.

Extreme Forensics. ID Discovery, 2010, "Playing with Fire" Episode 10, Season 2. TV series episode.

Forensic Files. Court TV, 2006, "Hot on the Trail" Episode 37, Season 10. TV series episode.

Jamieson, Dave. "Letter from an Arsonist." *Washington City Paper*, 2007.

---. "Why Thomas Sweatt Set Washington on Fire." *Washington City Paper*, 8 June 2007.

John Leonard Orr. *Points of Origin - Playing with Fire*. Haverford, Pa, Infinity Pub.com, 2001.

Luckett, Robert. Case Files (2003-2007).

"Md. Man Pleads Guilty Following Subdivision Arson." *Insurance Journal*, 27 June 2005, www.insurancejournal.com/news/east/2005/06/28/56710.htm.

National Center for the Analysis of Violent Crime. "Report of Essential Findings from a Study of Serial Arsonists | Office of Justice Programs." Www.ojp.gov, Department of Justice, 1994, www.ojp.gov/ncjrs/virtual-library/abstracts/report-essential-findings-study-serial-arsonists. Quantico, Virginia. FBI Academy #149950.

Nordskog, Ed. *"Torchered" Minds: Case Histories of Notorious Serial Arsonists.* Bloomington, In, Xlibris Corporation, 2011.

---. *The Arsonist Profiles: Analyzing Arson Motives and Behavior.* CreateSpace Independent Publishing Platform, 18 Aug. 2016.

"Paul Kenneth Keller." *Criminal Minds Wiki,* criminalminds.fandom.com/wiki/Paul_Kenneth_Keller.

Portrait of a Serial Arsonist: The Paul Keller Story. Directed by Michael Lienau, Global Net Productions, 1993.

Riffe, Jonathan. *Thomas Sweatt: Inside the Mind of DC's Most Notorious Arsonist.* Herndon, Virginia, Mascot Books, 2018.

Source Wikipedia. *American Arsonists: Lisa Lopes, Richard Hell, David Berkowitz, Kenny Richey, Ted Maher, Joseph Massino, Rod Coronado, Joseph Paul Franklin, Ottis Toole.* Memphis, Tennessee, Books, LLC (Wiki Series, 30 Aug. 2011.

United States Department of the Treasury. Bureau Of Alcohol, Tobacco, And Firearms. *Arson Case Briefs 1996.* Washington, DC, Bureau Of Alcohol, Tobacco, And Firearms, 1996.

United States Fire Administration. "2016 National Arson Awareness Week: Prevent Wildfire Arson." U.S. Fire Administration, 2016, www.usfa.fema.gov/prevention/outreach/wildfire_arson/.

United States Fire Administration (FEMA), et al. *U.S. Fire Administration/Technical Report Series Special Report: Firefighter Arson Homeland Security.* Jan. 2003.

Wambaugh, Joseph. *Fire Lover.* New York, N.Y., Harper Collins, 2002.

Wikipedia Contributors. "David Berkowitz." *Wikipedia*, Wikimedia Foundation, 6 May 2019, en.wikipedia.org/wiki/David_Berkowitz. Accessed 2020.

---. "Hunters Brooke Arson." *Wikipedia*, Wikimedia Foundation, 17 Sept. 2020, en.wikipedia.org/wiki/Hunters_Brooke_arson.

---. "John Leonard Orr." *Wikipedia*, Wikimedia Foundation, 7 Oct. 2019, en.wikipedia.org/wiki/John_Leonard_Orr. Accessed 2020.

---. "List of United States Federal Prisons." *Wikipedia*, Wikimedia Foundation, 15 July 2021, en.wikipedia.org/wiki/United_States_Penitentiary.

---. "Paul Kenneth Keller." *Wikipedia*, Wikimedia Foundation, 5 Apr. 2019, en.wikipedia.org/wiki/Paul_Kenneth_Keller. Accessed 2020.

---. "Thomas Sweatt." *Wikipedia*, Wikimedia Foundation, 25 Apr. 2020, en.wikipedia.org/wiki/Thomas_Sweatt.

ABOUT THE AUTHOR

ROBERT LUCKETT has worked in the public safety profession for more than four decades. His career has spanned both the fire service and law enforcement. He has held positions as a paramedic, fire inspector, 911 supervisor, assistant emergency manager, fire marshal, crime scene investigator, and custody officer. Luckett was the Chief Deputy Fire Marshal for the Alexandria Virginia Fire Department during the investigation.

Throughout his professional career, Luckett has served as an instructor and mentor. He has taught and lectured for the Virginia Fire Marshal Academy, the Virginia Department of Fire Programs, the Ocean City, Maryland Police Department, and the Eastern Shore Criminal Justice Academy. Bob has been awarded several commendations and awards for his work over the years.

He has been married to his wife, Caryn, for forty four years. They live in Fenwick Island, Delaware. Luckett played center on the TC Williams Titans football team made famous in the Disney movie *Remember the Titans*.

CPSIA information can be obtained
at www.ICGtesting.com
Printed in the USA
BVHW042114091221
623709BV00014B/798